Memoirs of WOMEN IN BLUE

THE GOOD, THE BAD AND NO LONGER SILENT

BY
MICKEY SEE-ASIA AND RAVEN

Publisher: MBK Enterprises, LLC
Publication Date: 2017
©2017 by Mickey See-Asia and Raven   All Rights Reserved
Printed in USA
ISBN-10:0-9971687-5-7
ISBN-13:978-0-9971687-5-4

Library of Congress Control Number: 2017905395

Edited by: Jay Polmar - Speed Read America
Design, Layout and Graphics by Becky Norwood
Cover Design by: Angie Ayala

Acknowledgements

To God we give ALL the glory, for without you, we are non-existing, failing to thrive. Thank you for carrying us safely through life's endeavors and giving us the ability, fortitudes, desires and strengths to share our experiences so that others may learn.

To our families and friends, we humbly appreciate the love, support, patience and encouragement you have given us as we have penned our thoughts. Thanks for the additional motivation to get our memoirs completed. Multitudes of blessings go to each one of you.

To Raven, my Co-Author, thank-you for coming to me with the idea of writing this memoir, holding me accountable, having patience and seeing our "Law Enforcement Memoirs," in its final printed stages.

To Mickey See-Asia, I especially thank you for being my Co-Author. Without your endless encouragement, these memoirs would not have been made possible.

Dedications

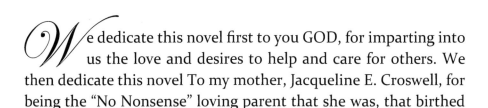

We dedicate this novel first to you GOD, for imparting into us the love and desires to help and care for others. We then dedicate this novel To my mother, Jacqueline E. Croswell, for being the "No Nonsense" loving parent that she was, that birthed the spiritual, mental and physical characters in me.

To my sibling brother's, we must continue to teach others what, MA taught us, for it is her legacy, "to love one another despite our differences and never hate."

I love you guys with All of my being.

To my God sisters- I just can't imagine this thing we call life without you being there. Whether near or far, WE ARE SISTERS FOR LIFE!!!!!!!!

To my son and daughter-in-law, birthing you son and then watching you and your beautiful wife mature into the wonderful adults that you are is only a reflection of me and my mother's impartation into you. Thank you for helping me be the best parent

I could be. It has not always been easy, but it has been definitely worth it. Most of All thank you for my beautiful granny babies.

To MM, thank you for being my "Boo Radley" throughout my entire life.

Thanks to All my family, extended family and friends, that I did not mention, for your love and continued support. You all play a significant role in my life....

With Great Admiration- Mickey See-Asia

I dedicate these memoirs to the families who have lost loved ones at the hands of police officers who have exercised poor judgment. To those who seek understanding in the tragedies that occur at an almost daily pace. I further dedicate these words to our future generation in the hopes that our communities will be a better place to live. To my children and grandchildren who through love and understanding, will make this world, a better place to live.

With Continued Love and Sincerity- Raven

Note to Readers

These words were not written to entertain the curious but to raise the level of awareness within the minds of our communities. This book is not intended to incite or make angry those who are disappointed with the way the public is policed, but to educate and bring knowledge and reason to situations that puzzle our society.

These memoirs expose the reader to the realities faced by female police officers who for years have remained silent at a time when the public needs so desperately to interpret the senseless acts of violence that are occurring on an almost daily basis across the country. Women are becoming more visible in law enforcement thus exposing them to more violence and intense pressures than what their male counterparts are confronted with. This elevates the risk factor for female officers to become involved in shootings, injuries or deaths. Unless a solution is offered and implemented quickly, more bloodshed will occur at the hands of those individuals who took an oath to protect the public.

This book contains the experiences of two female police detectives (one retired and the other resigned), from New York City Police Department, who have seen much, experienced good as well as evil and faced much opposition from their peers both male and female. On occasion, these officers also encountered some opposition from people in the various communities where they patrolled. These two women come from different socio-cultural backgrounds and offer you an inside look at what they observed and lived while trying to protect the public and dealt with the politics that governed how police officers should act while in the performance of their duty.

This sometimes biased, yet raw, look at what they lived through in their daily work lives should serve to remind you that situations should never be taken for granted and the need for a full examination is crucial to a well-informed and unbiased conclusion.

It is the authors' desire that you reach into your hearts and try to understand both perspectives, keep an open mind as you read these memoirs and take care not to jump quickly into judgment as you well understand that individual perceptions differ between persons. Keep in mind that situations change very quickly and not everyone is able to adapt resulting in oftentimes fatal consequences.

Table of Contents

Mickeys Memoirs

CHAPTER 1

Adult Actions That Can Leave Lifetime Impressions on Children

Where does one begin with a story or situation that appears to have a never-ending resolution?

Let me begin with ME.

As a young child, I was raised in a very culturally diversified neighborhood in the "Park Slope" section of Brooklyn, New York in the late 1950s through the early 1970s.

For the most part, the parents looked out for each other's children and we were extended family in that community. All the children played well together. Of course, we had our differences and fights but when the fights were over, we'd be back to being best friends.

In this community, most of the children would play in the Children's Park, which was located about half of a block from the Fire Department and around the corner from the local Police precinct.

For me and my friends to have access to this park we would have to walk from our homes two blocks away, passing by the local precinct. It was during my walks to this park with my friends that I encountered some long-term fearful memories of our friendly neighborhood Police Officers.

As my friends and I walked to the park one day there were several Officers standing on the steps of the Precinct. One of the Officers yelled out pointing to my friend Nancy, who was Caucasian, stating, "What are you doing with those coons? Don't let me see you playing with them anymore! Now you get on home, you hear!!!"

Nancy ran all the way back home while the rest of us, who were children of color, stood looking at the Officers not knowing what we had done wrong. "Now the rest of you monkeys, get on out of here and don't let me see you around here again or I'll lock you up and throw away the key! Get out of here!!!"

We scattered like roaches in all directions. Some of us made it to the Children's Park, while others did just as Nancy had done, ran home. Needless to say, my friends and I found an alternate way to the park without passing in front of the precinct.

Later that day I told my mother what had happened. She became very angry and wanted to go to the precinct to speak with the person in charge. Her husband told her that it was not a good idea and suggested that it should be chalked up as a lesson learned. My siblings and I were instructed to never walk past that precinct again.

I asked my mother what a "coon" was and why the police officer called us "monkeys." She explained that the words "coon" and "monkeys" were bad names that the police and some Caucasian people used to describe people of color.

As inquisitive as I was, I continued to ask questions because I really did not understand the actions of that police officer, nor the responses of the other officers standing on the steps with him. They were laughing at us while the other officer screamed and threatened us.

All of the officers were Caucasian. My mother simply replied, "Those police officers were mean and bad police officers." She explained that there are good and bad people that I will encounter in my life. She stated that I must pray for both and forgive the bad. I reminded Mother that she had trained my siblings and me that if we were ever lost that we should try to find a police officer so they could bring us safely home. After this incident, I didn't want to deal with any police officers...good or bad!!!

My mother and I then went to visit with our neighbors, Nancy and her parents. While Nancy and I hugged, and played together, our mothers had a very long conversation out of hearing distance.

CHAPTER 2

Wanting to Make a Difference

everal years went by, and after I had my beautiful, bubbly baby boy, I decided that working two jobs was time consuming and keeping me from bonding with my child. I applied for the Civil Service Police Officer position for the New York City Police Department. It was 1979.

I thought long and hard after taking the exam about why I wanted to become a police woman on the streets of NYC. Why did I want to put my life on the line like that, knowing that I was a single mom with much ambition, drive and determination? There were so many things I could have done with my life.

But somewhere in the back of my mind I kept seeing and hearing those police officers from my childhood. The ones calling me "coon" and "monkey" and threatening my friends and for no other reason other than that I was African American. The more I thought of that, the more I knew I needed to be a police officer in the community. One who worked towards helping in the community, being a mentor for the children, being a positive role model for others so that that the community would know that I was truly committed to the task of "protecting and serving."

Once I took the exam, which I had passed with a very high score, I was called in 1980 to initiate the candidate processing. There were several phases to the processing.

Candidates were required to take a pre-medical, full medical, psychological, background investigation and a physical agility test. We were required to pass each phase in order to move onto the next phase.

I passed the pre-med with flying colors. I had some concerns as to whether I would pass the weight and height requirements. At that time, in the summer of 1980, I was told that I should be no less than 125 pounds and a height of at least 5 feet 7 inches. My weight was 122 pounds. I had always been very athletically inclined, so I believed in myself that I would do well and pass all the phases of the candidate processing.

I had three weeks before I was required to take my full medical, so I had to put some weight on in the right way and in the right proportions, while preparing myself physically for the physical agility portion of the process. My mind and heart were now set on becoming a police woman and I was doing everything in my power, very determined to achieve my goal.

I prayed that God would grant me this job so that I could be one that would and could make a difference in people's lives. I started jogging again, (I ran track as a pre-teen and teenager) and I even hired a personal trainer.

When it was time for my full medical, I passed with no set-backs. I was then assigned a police investigator who would conduct my background investigation.

The background investigation entailed reviewing and interviewing those from my employment history who could attest to my character and education history. They checked on my criminal background, which I did not have. They also checked on my credit history. My entire life, at age 23, was an open book and I had nothing to hide.

My investigator used to state, "I wish all of my candidate's background histories was as easy to retrieve, with no negative incidents to report as yours is!" To my knowledge, I had no derogatory information in my past, so I was passing each phase of the candidate process with a breeze, except for passing the driving requirements.

As a police cadet candidate, I was required to have a New York State driver's license, which I did not have. As a native New Yorker growing up in the city, there was no need for me to have a car because there was always mass transit. Buses, trains, cabs, and ferries were always available to get around in the five boroughs. A car was a luxury that I really did not think about prior to becoming a police officer. I took some driving lessons and after failing it a few times, I finally received my license.

I was then scheduled for my psychological written exam. This exam was a variety of nearly 1000 questions, some of which were re-worded in different sections of the exam. On each section of the exam, the candidates were given a time limit to complete as many questions in that section as possible in the allotted time period. I believe that the re-wording of some of the questions was to see if the candidates were consistent with their answers.

There were only one of two answers you could use in answering questions...yes or no. I completed all of the sections in a timely manner, but did ponder over one question that was re-worded differently in a least three sections. To the best of my recollection, the questions were asked in the following manner: "Will you love your mother?" To which I responded, "Yes." "Can you love your mother?" I answered, "Yes." "Did you love your mother?" I answered, "No."

The reason I answered no was because of my perception of this question was that it was asking me in the past tense, meaning that my mother was deceased, did I love her. My mother was not deceased at the time, so I put the answer as no.

With the test completed, I was ready for the next phase of the processing...the physical agility phase. During this phase you were required to complete a specific amount of push-ups, pull-ups, sit-ups, jumping jacks, squats, climbing an A-frame wall, climbing a five-foot wall and completing a two-mile run. This had to be completed in a certain time frame based on the candidate's weight and height. I breezed through each section and passed with flying colors. As I watched other candidates performing their tasks for agility, I noticed that many of the top heavy or bottom heavy women had difficulties climbing a five-foot wall and doing the allotted amount of push-ups and pull-ups required for them to pass that section.

After passing the physical agility tests, I only had the oral psychological test, as well as having my investigator finalize my background investigation. I was prepared for the upcoming January 1982 cadet class!

I was contacted to come in for my oral psychological test, not knowing what to expect other than to be questioned about my answers to the written psych exam I'd taken a few months prior.

Upon entering the Psychologist's office, I was directed to have a seat by a female's voice with a squeaky tone. I observed a desk and a big swivel chair with the back of the chair facing me and another chair in front of the desk, which I assumed I was to be seated in. I sat in silence for what seemed an eternity, when a female voice said to me from behind the back of the chair, (I had not had the opportunity to have a face to face with the voice at this time); "So you think you want to be a New York City Police Officer?"

I had no idea if this was some kind of trick question or what. If you can imagine being in my shoes, try to visualize the scenario! There I was sitting in a room, staring at the back of a high top chair, waiting to make eye contact with the voice behind the chair. I kept my composure and I stated, "Yes, I know I would like to be a NYPD officer upon completion of my candidate processing."

The voice then asks me, "Why should you be selected above any other candidate?" To which I responded, "Because I believe I am the best suitable and qualified for the position as a police woman for the NYPD." Then there was silence...for about a minute, a minute that seemed like an eternity. A minute spent sitting there looking at the back of that high top brown leather chair, in anticipation of meeting the voice. It appeared that the voice I was hearing was coming from a very high pitched tone woman who may have been a relatively small or mid-sized woman.

Nevertheless, whoever the voice was, she was apparently the psychologist and my task was just to answer the questions that were presented to me regardless of whether I got to see her face or not.

The next question took me totally off guard. The voice asked in an even higher pitched tone, "According to your test question, you don't like your mother. Why?" Again, I sat staring at the back of that chair, wondering how she came to that conclusion from my test results. I thought before I answered and stated, "I love my mother, I may not like some of the things she does sometimes, but I love her very much." To which she responded, "That's not what you said on your test questions. You clearly indicated that you do not love your mother!!!"

I then recalled the three questions that I had pondered over the wording of in the written psychological test. "Will you love your mother?" I answered yes. "Can you love your mother?" I had answered yes. "Did you love your mother?" I had answered no. I explained the reason that I had stated "no" to the question, was that the question appeared to be a past-tense question that required a yes or no answer with no elaboration, and I knew that my mother was not deceased. She was very much alive and I love her very much. Even if and when she expires I will always love her.

The voice then asked, "Then why didn't you just respond yes as you did with the other questions about your mother?" I again repeated, "For the above reasons stated."

I really began to feel that this psychologist was looking for a reason to fail me. The voice requested that I tell her about my childhood. Because I did not want to go into details and possibly be discriminated against because of things that happened in my childhood, I expressed that I had two brothers, my mother and father and a dog and that we lived in a three level home with separate apartments. I expressed that it was a culturally diversified community and I had many friends of different ethnic backgrounds.

As I finished my statement, I observed the back of the chair slowly oscillating around and what I saw sitting in that chair face to face was exactly what I had expected, a dwarf-sized Caucasian woman with little hands and a large head. The woman I saw did not change my thought process, I know she was credentialed to be conducting that interview and it was my responsibility to be courteous and respectful and answer the questions accordingly.

The psychologist then stated, "Thank you for your time," and she dismissed me. Prior to exiting I inquired if I would be getting the results in the mail and she responded, "Your investigator will contact you." I thanked her and that concluded the interview. I left there not knowing whether I passed or failed.

CHAPTER 3

Anticipation

*L*ife went on. I was working as a bank teller and nurturing my son as a single mom. A few months had passed from the time I had the oral psychological and I had not heard anything from my Investigator or anyone from NYPD.

I heard advertisements on the radio for the upcoming Police Academy Class scheduled for January 1982, so I attempted to contact my Investigator to learn of my current status.

What I did learn was that my Investigator was no longer in the unit and it was unknown at the time just who my current Investigator was.

It was the beginning of December 1981, and I contacted the Applicant Processing Unit and was informed by the officer who was assisting me, that it was unknown who my Investigator was, but it appeared that I had been placed on investigative and psych review, which was detaining me from going into the upcoming January 1982, academy class.

I inquired with the officer on how I could ascertain why I was placed on investigative review and I was referred to a unit called the "Retention Unit." I did not know at the time but this referral was the best thing that could have happened to me because it opened doors years later in my life.

It was the Christmas Holiday Season and it was truly difficult striving to get answers on how I could clear up my Investigative/Psych review status.

Unfortunately, I missed the January 1982, Academy Class, due to my pending review status. I was disheartened about that decision but I had to keep it moving along. I did not give up. There was another upcoming Police Officer Civil Service exam and it was my intention to take that exam as well, so that I kept my options open.

Several months passed and I received a call from a Police Officer from the Retention Unit. His name I will not reveal, but his actions and his efforts as my Retention Officer went far and beyond getting me hired by NYPD.

The officer educated me on the purpose of his call which was to assist in getting me properly and rightfully hired by NYPD. He apologized for my missing the prior class but his goal was to get me ready and qualified for the future academy class. He did advise that several hundred other people of color had been placed on either investigative review, psych review or both, prior to the January 1982 academy class without proper justification.   He advised in my background investigation there was nothing in my records to warrant me being placed on investigative review.

He stated he did find a letter from the psychologist indicating that I should be placed on psych review for a second opinion by another NYPD Psychologist. The officer did advise that the psychologist who did the oral exam had a record of either failing or placing "people of color" on psych review.

The Retention Officer set up an appointment for me to conduct a face-to-face visit with him regarding my files in his office.

I arrived at the Retention Unit which was located at that time at 346 Broadway, NY, on my assigned date and time. It was a nice hot summer day. I sat down with the Retention Unit Officer and he educated me on what I should do in reference to the Psychologist's letter of review. He gave me a copy and directed me to be seen by an outside psychiatrist or psychologist and have he or she evaluate me based on my past and present family and employment history.

The Officer explained the reason that I was placed on Investigatory Review and not Psych review, was because my file had not been deemed as 3Q (qualified medically, psychologically and Investigative) and my prior Investigator had been reassigned months prior to the January 1982 class.

So, my file just sat in a pile of unattended and unassigned cases, with no disposition. So the closer it got to the 1982 class these unassigned/unattended cases had to be accounted for in some way, so they were marked as either Investigative or Psych review prior to the class and not considered for the Academy class.

The Retention Officer advised he would do his best in getting my file re-assigned to a new Investigator and in the meantime, I would have to work on getting a Psych evaluation from an Independent Therapist, Psychiatrist or Psychologist.

I also informed the Officer that I was scheduled to take the next upcoming Civil Service Police Officer Exam, which he commended me for doing. I then inquired, "How would my Psych or Investigative Review, (I still did not understand why I was on Investigative Review), affect my chances of being hired from the new exam? The Officer advised, "Let's cross that bridge if you should get to that point."

I thanked the Officer for his assistance and advice and left the building.

I went on with life as usual, raising my son as a single mom and working. I was able to locate a wonderful family therapist and psychiatrist on Central Park West in Manhattan, NY.

I attended three (3) sessions with this psychiatrist and he felt that there was no need for any additional sessions. He did not find that I was psychiatrically unfit in anyway, he felt quite the contrary. He advised, from his observation and review of my background history, that I would make a very responsible, caring and dedicated officer.

I was able to retrieve a copy of his assessment and I requested that he forward his assessment to the psychologist who evaluated me in NYPD. I made an appointment with my Retention Unit Officer to bring him a copy of the assessment as well.

I took the next NYPD Civil Service exam, and aced it with a score of 100. I was very proud of myself when I received those results.

My family was also very proud of me. They were my support system, encouraging me not to give up and continue to pursue my dreams. My mother was especially supportive, not only was she there for me, she was there helping to raise my son.

My mother knew how disappointed I was when I did not make it into the last Police Academy.

When she learned of the reasons why I was put on review because of the psych question, "Did you love you mother?" She asked, "What kind of trick question is that? I'm not dead." She asked me what did I put as the answer and I told her, I could only answer yes or no, no explanations were allowed, and I answered it as, "No". Mama stated, "You could have answered that question with both a yes and no answer, and they would both be correct as long as you could provide a valid explanation." I told Mama, "I did just that during the oral interview, explained why I stated 'no' because my mother was not deceased and it appeared that the NYPD psychologist was not satisfied with my answer."

That is the reason why I had to seek help from the Retention Unit and an outside psychiatrist.

CHAPTER 4

The Call

*A*nother year rolled in, 1983. I was claiming this as my year to be hired by NYPD.

In or around March of 1983, I received a call from my Retention Union Officer, who provided me with information and a scheduled date. He provided me with my oral psych review date and the telephone number to my new Investigator. He advised once I had my oral interview and met with my new Investigator I was to contact him.

A week later I met with my new Investigator and provided him with the updated information he had requested during our telephone conference. Two weeks after I met with my Investigator I had my psych oral review, which was totally different from the initial psych oral.

The oral review consisted of a panel of psychiatrists or psychologists that asked a slew of questions in regard to my childhood upbringing, family, friends, school and employment. I walked out of that review feeling very confident.

In May 1983, I was contacted and congratulated by both my Investigator and my Retention Unit Officer, informing me that I was qualified for the upcoming Academy class, scheduled for July 25, 1983.

I was very proud of myself, excited and looking forward to the challenges of becoming a New York City Police Woman.

My family and friends were very excited for me as well. I was the second in my immediate family to become a Police Officer and the first female in my family to become a Police Woman.

I did have an Aunt who married into the family, who was a Housing Police Officer for a few years prior to me becoming a NYPD Police Officer, who I had the opportunity after I was assigned to my precinct, to interact and patrol within the Brownsville section of Brooklyn.

CHAPTER 5

The Police Academy

⟳

I joined the ranks of New York's Finest, Police Cadets on July 25, 1983. We were not called Cadets in 1983, we were called rookies. The first day of the academy was truly hectic. First we all took the oath and were sworn in as rookies to do our very best, so that when we graduated we would take the Oath to Serve & Protect those in our communities as Police Officers.

We were assigned to our companies (classes), learned the cadences for NYPD, we had to run through the Police Academy, while we wore our rookie gear and carried academic books. Academy Black duffle bags were literally thrown at us as we ran to each level in The Police Academy.

I believe my Academy company class was 83-72, or something very similar to that. We had to select a company president (class president). We were advised to select someone who had military background and could lead the company in cadence and throughout our five month academy class. We were scheduled to graduate from the Academy by the end of December 1983.

On our first day when the companies were called to gather in certain areas of the Academy, to "Muster" as it was called, different Police Instructors educated us on what to expect. One of the instructors continuously referred to the rookies as "Whale Shit." He informed us that we were below the status of rookies, we were wet behind the ears, couldn't smell or find ourselves out of a hole if we had to, and we were to address and salute him as, "Yes, Sir, Yes."

This instructor found one of the rookies to pick on and continued to call the rookie some choice words throughout the day. The rookie would turn red in the face every time this instructor would get directly in front of him, look him in the face and scream at him as loud as he could, sometimes with saliva coming out of his mouth while screaming. My thoughts were, "please don't let this idiot find his way to me and scream at me for no reason at all." Thank God that did not happen.

What we did learn though, later that first day was the rookie who was being picked on, was the son of one of the high ranking Chiefs of Department.

Needless to say, when we returned to the Academy on our second day, we had a brief gathering called a "Mustering" of companies on the first floor.

We were greeted and welcomed by several high ranking Chiefs in the Police Dept. The next encounter that we had was, the Police Instructor who called us "Whale Shit" and was picking on the rookie the day before, was called up to speak to all of us rookies.

He apologized for his behavior the day before and he apologized for calling us the inappropriate names that he called us. The Chief's son was also called up to where the Instructor was and the Instructor saluted the rookie with "Yes, Sir, Yes" and apologized for treating him in the manor that he had treated him the day before. I know that had to be very humiliating for that Instructor.

The Chief of Department then explained to us that although we were rookies we were part of a unified para-military family and we should not be disrespected, especially by our own kind. They started brain washing us early in the training that we were "Brothers and Sisters in Blue" and that "we had to have each other's backs."

The next few months were intense with academic classes consisting of social science, police science, law, cultural diversity, agility, driving obstacle courses and firearms training.

Every two months were bi-monthly exams that would move us to the next level. For those who did not pass these exams they were given an opportunity to retake it, and if they failed a second time they were dismissed from the academy.

During several of our academic training classes one of the instructors, would reminisce about his experiences as a patrol officer, and he always spoke about how important it was for police officers to look out for one another and to have each other's back when no one else would.

He emphasized that "we were now one big family, more unified then our blood family." He gave an example as, "If we as police officers responded to a job, and one of your blood family members happened to be involved in some way with the 911 call, regardless to the circumstances, we as police officers had to protect each other, before we would consider protecting our blood family.

He stated, even if it resulted in our blood family being injured, we were to bifurcate our feelings for that family member and protect our fellow officers." I never felt comfortable, nor did I agree with that statement for many reasons.

He also discussed with the class about the "Blue Wall of Silence," making sure we understood how important it was for us never to disclose or tell on another officer. He indicated that there would be times that we as police officers would need the assistance of our fellow officers and the last thing that any officer would want to be labeled as was a "rat" or one that went against the grain.

Ethically, I never agreed with what I was told during this training session. But unfortunately, even after I graduated from the academy, I learned and experienced more about "The Blue Wall of Silence" that still exists to this very day.

As a rookie in the Academy, I had no idea or no true sense about what this "Blue Wall of Silence" meant to a police officer, especially if he/she was caught in a certain situation; how truly devastating it could be if one did not have the ethical values or morals to make appropriate decisions on what's right and what's wrong.

During my tenure as a rookie in the Academy, one of my challenges, as well as challenges for other "Persons of Color" in the Academy were dealing with some of the Caucasian knucklehead rookies who lacked the cultural diversity and made many disparaging remarks about other ethnic groups during role play, or during our cultural diversity class.

They just didn't get it. They generalized making statements such as, "You people don't have the skills or knowledge, you're undereducated" or better yet they would state, "I never had to deal with you people in my community."

Imagine that. In the 1980s you had Caucasian people who had never dealt with people of color, who were hired into NYPD's finest, and they were going to protect and serve, WHO & HOW?

These rookies did not even realize that they were being offensive by utilizing the terminology, "You people."

Our Cultural Diversification training instructor educated them that their offensive language could escalate any situation to a point of arrest or physical injury unnecessarily.

There were three of these knuckleheads that traveled together in our academy company. As much as we discussed, conducted role plays, and collectively expressed to these rookies the importance of educating and interacting with other cultures, especially because of the type of job that they had chosen to be part of, they did not feel that they needed to make any changes in their lifestyles.

Two out of the three did graduate with the company. The third did not pass the academics and was dismissed from the academy. I have no idea what happened to the other two after graduation, but I'm certain they probably wound up with numerous IAD complaints of abuse of authority, especially against people of color.

The Academy training continued and our academic instructor, (the one who reminisced about his policing days quite frequently) continuously discussed the importance of police officers having each other's back, no matter what the situation.

As a rookie, I felt very uncomfortable with this instructor continuously expressing this statement and then following up with the "Blue Wall of Silence." I took the liberty to learn more about what this blue wall of silence was, and I learned the following:

"The Blue Wall of Silence, also Blue Code and Blue Shield, are terms used to denote the unwritten rule that exists among police officers not to report on a colleague's errors, misconducts, or crimes. If questioned about an incident of misconduct involving another officer (e.g. during an official inquiry), while following the code, the officer being questioned would claim ignorance of another officer's wrongdoing.

The code is considered to be police corruption and misconduct. Any officers who engage in discriminatory arrests, physical or verbal harassment, and selective enforcement of the law are considered to be corrupt. Many officers who follow the code may participate in some of these acts during their career for personal matters or in order to protect or support fellow officers. All of these are considered illegal offenses and are grounds for suspension or immediate dismissal. Officers who follow the code are unable to report fellow officers who participate in corruption due to the unwritten laws of their 'police family.'" (Webster & Wikipedia).

One thing I knew for certain is I did not want anything to do with this "Blue Wall of Silence," and I prayed during my tenure as a cop that I would never be subjected to some other cop's buffoonery that would leave me no other recourse but to report him or her.

I was not going to jeopardize my life for the foolish mistakes of another, but I also had to recognize the downfall for telling the truth of my observations. It was a double-edge sword. Don't report and live with my conscience or report it and suffer the consequences. I decided I would choose the latter, knowing that I made the correct ethical decision for whatever the situation entailed.

I was learning in my infant days as a rookie what it was going to be like working with some of my fellow officers. I couldn't help but wonder if I made a right choice.

The Academy training class was soon coming to an end and we rookies were going to be assigned to what was called our "Neighborhood Stabilization Units," which was the rookies actual "on the job" training precincts. The rookie would work in the "NSU" for a period of six months alongside tenured police officers and learn the ropes of the job after graduating from the police academy.

The academy was true mental, physical and emotional training. If you had childlike thoughts when you came in, you left with an Adult Law Enforcement Officer state of mind, or at least you thought you did.

The NSU was the reinforcement that the rookies would utilize their book knowledge combined with their street knowledge that they would acquire from the various tenured officers they would patrol with during the NSU phase.

About a week before the police academy graduation, I learned that I would be patrolling the streets of Crown Heights, Flatbush, Canarsie, and Nostrand Avenue in Brooklyn during my six-month NSU training. I was happy that the academic portion of the police training was coming to end and I was preparing myself for the next stage of policing.

We rookies spent the last week at Madison Square Garden, where the actual graduation was to take place. We had to practice our marching ceremony at Madison Square Garden. There were approximately 2000 rookies that would be graduating from my academy class and we were marching into the Garden while one of New York's greatest songs was playing, which will be mentioned at a later time.

Believe it or not it did not take too many practices for our rookie academy class to get the song, cadence and salute together for the graduation.

Graduation day was a beautiful sight. The rookie's families were seated in the upper levels while the rookies, lined up in order by last name in the lower levels.

When the ceremony began we marched in so proudly in our "dress uniforms and white gloves," to Franks Sinatra's "New York, New York." I'm sure we made our families very proud in watching us march in, in unison and salute the American flag simultaneously.

As the ceremony went on throughout the morning we, the rookies, were edified by the hierarchy of the police department as well as by the political dignitaries that attended, the Mayor of New York being one of the dignitaries. During the ceremony, the rookies were directed to stand and raise their right hands, to collectively take the oath to "Protect and Serve."

As we stood together and raised our right hands, the Mayor directed us to repeat these words: "I do hereby pledge to declare, to uphold The Constitution of the United States, and The Constitution of the State of New York and will faithfully discharge my duties as a New York City Police Officer to the best of my ability, SO HELP ME GOD!"

The Mayor then congratulated us and the Police Commissioner said a few choice words.

The graduation was ending. At the end of the ceremony I looked around at my graduating class of approximately 2000 rookies, which consisted of a multitude of different cultures, noticing that the majority were Caucasian. My thoughts were then, "How many of these police officer rookies really believe in and will take this oath seriously?" I did not know!

CHAPTER 6

The Journey Begins

The first day of training at my NSU precinct, myself and two other rookies from the academy were introduced to the staff at the precinct.

We were assigned to field training officers, better known as FTO's and were required to have two days of in-house training and three days in the field shadowing senior officers.

In the precinct where I was assigned to perform my patrol NSU duties, the FTO taught us via videos that we had to be very careful of a specific group of people who were considered to be a threat to law enforcement officers and people in authority.

The FTO advised that the "self-proclaimed hate group were called Rastafarians." We rookies were shown all types of videos of "Rastas" as they were called.

The videos showed how "Rastas" stored various weapons in their dreadlock hairdo's or on their person. The rookies were educated on what to look for when encountering a "Rasta." The "Rastas" in the community had been known for their illegal sales and usage of "ganja", known as marijuana. In 1984 we were trained that not only were the "Rastas" selling the ganja but they were now manufacturing the new "crack" cocaine.

The FTO advised that in certain geographical areas of the community that were covered by the precinct, we were now in a "Drug War Zone." The "Rasta's," we were told, were fighting and killing each other and other people in the community for "turf", to sell and manufacture the drugs.

There were numerous different cultures residing in this community. You had a section where there were many "Islanders" as they were called (a person who originated in one of the Caribbean Islands, and migrated to Brooklyn, NY). There were various other ethnic groups and there were also the Lubavitcher Jewish people.

During this time, there was a lot of dissention between the cultural groups because some of the African American constituents in this community felt that the Jewish constituents were receiving preferential treatment above all other constituents and were not subjected to the same biased treatment that the "people of color" in the community were being subjected to.

Unfortunately, due to this "alleged preferential treatment" some people of color in the community stopped looking at the Jewish Community as allies, but as oppressors.

Being an African American police officer (rookie or senior) during this time, in this community, dealing with the disparities between ethnic groups was not an easy task. There was always one ethnic group or the other that felt that they were either better than the other ethnic groups and some of the African Americans in the community would be calling the African American officers "Uncle Toms," because they felt the officers failed to take specific actions against the other ethnic group.

I, as the rookie cop, did not concern myself with the race, creed or color of the people in the community. I truly believed in treating everyone fairly. I took an oath to Protect and Serve the **people** in the communities I patrolled, not just specific ethnic groups in that community.

I was learning fast that, there was some level of preferential treatment for certain ethnic groups that were designated by the hierarchy in NYPD, and as an officer (rookie or not), I had to follow the directives given. This, more than anything, caused confusion in my spirit whether to follow what I believed to be ethically correct or face the consequences of my actions for doing what I thought was the correct thing to do.

As stated in an Article from "Framing Identity: The Press in Crown Heights:"

"There were 'manifestations of other confrontations on six major issues: fairness in the distribution of community resources; fairness in the distribution of housing; police accommodations to the Lubavitchers; the perception of a "double standard" of the police in dealing with alleged crime; the Lubavitcher crime patrol; and the Hasidic ambulance service.

The African and Caribbean-American communities feel that they have been disadvantaged on all of these issues, and that the Lubavitchers receive preferential treatment. The Lubavitchers maintain that they must protect and exercise their rights as a minority in Crown Heights, including things that are pertinent to their religious tradition.'

The issue regarding police accommodations to the Lubavitchers is a particularly sensitive one for the African- and Caribbean-American communities. They contend that the Police

Department and the City have demonstrated a conspicuous pattern of "preferential treatment" toward the Lubavitchers.

The example they most often cite is the practice of closing public streets and barricading a service road during the Jewish Sabbath and on other Holy Days. This sometimes has resulted in bus and traffic rerouting, as well as identity checks of the residents in order to drive down the closed streets.

The Lubavitchers answer their critics by contending that this helps them to exercise their religious freedom, and that it also protects the safety of thousands of worshipers who fill the streets on Sabbaths and Holy Days.

People of African descent in Crown Heights believe that the Lubavitchers have a disproportionate share of political clout and therefore receive preferential treatment from the City government. This resentment is exacerbated by the traditions and culture of the Lubavitchers, which is highly insular, and limits dialogue.

For their part, the Lubavitchers contend that their distinctiveness and reticence makes them targets of robbery, bias crimes, and other forms of anti-Semitism. They maintain that they are a highly vulnerable minority group in the neighborhood."

As a rookie officer, I oftentimes had to walk a foot post in the Crown Heights community. On several day tours I was assigned to conduct foot patrol in the Lubavitchers section of the community, which generally was a quiet tour with no incidents to report. Prior to beginning my shift, I would be informed during roll call not to issue any summonses in the Lubavitchers Community.

As I walked the beat one spring morning I observed a vehicle that was double parked on a two-lane traffic moving street, one lane with southbound traffic and the other was northbound traffic. The motorist was not in the vehicle. The vehicle appeared to be a brand new vehicle and the problem was that it was blocking traffic.

The motorists in the moving vehicles were beeping their horns as they were forced to have to go around the doubled-parked vehicle, others were making disparaging comments as I radioed in to conduct a plate check on the vehicle. The plate came back as a "No Hit" meaning it was not listed as stolen and the owner of the vehicle resided in Staten Island.

I radioed in to have a Sergeant meet me at the location, "No Emergency".

I walked around the block a few times, 30 minutes passed with no Sergeant arriving to assist. The dispatcher advised that the Sergeant was on another call and would respond as soon as he could. The traffic was getting backed up because there were city buses that travelled this street and they were being detained because of this double-parked vehicle that had been sitting in traffic for over 45 minutes.

I know I was directed during roll call not to issue summonses in this community, but this motorist showed a flagrant disregard to the New York State vehicle traffic law, by double parking the vehicle on a busy city street and leaving the vehicle doubled parked for at least an hour that I observed.

I had to make a split decision. I did request assistance for a Sergeant and he had not responded.

I could have called for a tow truck to come and tow the vehicle, but instead I issued two summonses to the vehicle and continued to another section of my foot post.

Sometime during the mid-afternoon, the dispatcher was calling my foot post to return to the command. Upon my arrival to the precinct I was directed to meet with the Commanding Officer in his office.

The Union Representative at the precinct met with me before I had to meet with the CO and he informed me that some members from the Jewish Community were in the CO's Office with some summonses I had written earlier that day. I explained to the Union Representative everything that took place and the reason why the vehicle was given the summonses.

The Union Representative was present with me as I entered the CO's office, where I observed the CO and two gentlemen who appeared to be from the Lubavitch community. One appeared to be in his mid-twenties and the other around 50. Both were wearing the long black coats, black hats, white tassels, the elder had a beard.

The CO presented me with the summons and asked if I had written these summons, and I affirmed that I did. He directed me to void the summonses and reprimanded me in the presence of the gentlemen for writing the summonses.

After the two gentlemen exited the CO's office at the precinct, the Union Representative voiced to the CO that he felt that I should not have been reprimanded for doing my job appropriately.

He then explained to the CO as to what happened and why the summonses were issued. The CO stated that the gentlemen who had left the precinct were not only well known in the community but also had some political ties. The CO apologized for reprimanding me and advised that I did not have to walk a foot post in the Jewish Community again.

That did not do much for my pride, my feelings or the fact that I had done the right thing by issuing the summonses. I had to "suck it up" and continue business as usual.

I was placed in a Squad car for the better part of my rookie neighborhood stabilization unit days at that precinct or I was temporarily reassigned for the day to another precinct.

It was during my temporary reassignment to a precinct in a predominantly Caucasian neighborhood that I encountered my second lifetime experience at being called a racially derogatory name, even while in my uniform. This event also involved an improperly parked vehicle blocking traffic.

As I walked the beat in the Canarsie Section of Brooklyn, I observed a vehicle that was tripled parked on a very busy city street. Instead of automatically issuing a summons to the vehicle, I first took the time to visit the many merchandise shops and restaurants that lined the streets in search of the owner of the vehicle. I stopped and inquired in every store and no one claimed the vehicle.

I walked back to the vehicle and called in on my radio for a plate check. After receiving confirmation that the vehicle was not stolen, I retrieved the name and address of the owner of the vehicle. I also called for a tow truck to tow the vehicle to the City pound because the vehicle was causing traffic back-up.

As I began to write the summons, a Caucasian woman came running out of the restaurant that I had just exited. She was screaming all types of expletives as she ran towards me when I placed the summons on her vehicle. I directed the woman to stop and compose herself before she created additional problems for herself.

The woman continued to scream, curse and make a scene to the point that she was drawing a crowd. I saw that the crowd was growing, and it appeared that the majority of the crowd was angry at me for issuing the summons. As I placed the summons on the vehicle, I called for assistance on the radio.

I took a step away from the car, while calmly directing the outraged woman to compose herself. She then stated, "We don't need no N-word cop, coming into our neighborhood, writing tickets and creating problems."

Things got heated very quickly and I found myself surrounded by the crowd. The woman took her summons and ripped it up. She retained the shredded summons in her hand and took a step into my personal space as I stepped back.

I advised her that she was inciting a riot and if she did not quietly leave the scene, she would be arrested for inciting. It seemed like an eternity for my back-up to arrive and I did not want to make an arrest in the middle of an angered crowd.

Apparently, she did not take me seriously and continued to taunt me and then threw the shredded summons at me. I again calmly advised her to step on the side of her car and I notified her she was being issued another summons for littering.

Well that statement just sent her overboard, I stepped back, she stepped forward making a charging movement towards me.

One thing I was satisfied to know was that the particular academy training I learned for this type of situation was very successful. I was able to subdue her and get her cuffed, at the same time multitudes of back-up arrived on the scene.

The surrounding crowd spread open like the "Red Sea", when my fellow officers arrived. I was very happy and relieved to see them on the scene. I placed my perp (female motorist) in the rear of the RMP (police vehicle) and I sat in the front passenger seat and "Mirandized" my perp while we were transported back to the precinct to process the paper work for my first arrest.

We rookies learned in both the academy and NSU training any time you cuffed and interrogated a perp you were required to read them their rights which is called "Miranda Warnings or Miranda Rights and notate the perp's response in our Memo Books.

The Miranda Warning is stated as follows:

"You have the right to remain silent. Anything you say can and will be used against you in a court of law. You have the right to an attorney. If you cannot afford an attorney, one will be provided for you. Do you understand the rights I have just read to you? With these rights in mind, do you wish to speak to me?"

If looks could kill I would have been a dead officer in the front of that RMP. As I looked back to inform my perp of her rights, her eyes were rolling and she cussed me from A-Z saying, "I'm gonna have your job."

I informed Ms. Jane Doe, that she was being charged with the following NY State Penal Code charges, Aggravated assault upon a police officer or a peace officer, B Violent Felony, 120.11., and Aggravated Inciting to Riot, an A Misdemeanor, 240.08.

My perp and I were transported back to the precinct where, Jane Doe was placed in a holding cell while I completed the arrest process and paperwork. Jane Doe actually became very quiet and cooperative once she was placed in the cell.

The senior officer was assigned to assist me with my first arrest. I fingerprinted Jane Doe, let her make a phone call and explained to her what the process was. Once I completed her paperwork, she was going to be transported to Central Booking where she would be processed for arraignment to meet with a judge.

I am certain that Jane Doe would think twice on how she approached any Police Officer in future interactions with the law.

CHAPTER 7

My Patrol Unit Precinct

After my NSU days at the Crown Height's precinct, I was assigned to a precinct in East New York. My first few weeks at the precinct, I was debriefed and trained about the various sections of East New York that were considered hazardous to an Officer's life.

My work schedule at that time varied and rotated. In one month's schedule, I worked from 8 a.m. through 4 p.m., for one week, then I worked two consecutive weeks of 4 p.m. through 12 a.m., and the last week would be a graveyard shift, 12 a.m. through 8 a.m. Initially it was rough adapting to this schedule. As a NSU rookie, we were not required to perform mid-night shifts, just 8x4's and 4x12's. Now I was termed to be a Patrol Cop, so welcome to the real world of policing.

My observations of the officers in the precinct, were that there was division in the precinct. I would say 70% of the officers were

Caucasian, 20% were African Americans and 10% were made up of other ethnic backgrounds. While on breaks and in the precinct most of the ethnic groups stayed within their groups.

But when roll call took place it did not matter what ethnic group we were, you took your assignment and we were supposed to be all on the same team, "Brothers and Sisters in Blue!!"

My first few months went by pretty smoothly as one of the new rookies in the precinct. I walked a lot of foot posts with other rookie officers and one senior officer showing us the ropes. Most tenured officers were in radio cars as the newer officers walked the beat. I enjoyed being on a foot post because I got to interact with the people in the community. As a rookie in the Crown Heights Precinct, I spent many days on a foot post, so it prepared me for my foot patrol in the E.N.Y Precinct. I was very people oriented and people friendly so it did not take long for me to befriend the store owners and constituents in the community where I walked the beat.

My very first encounter being in a radio car was a very memorable one. During roll call on a 4x12 shift, I was assigned to ride in the RMP (Radio Motorized Patrol Car as they were called) with the Sr. Officer who had a few years under his belt. I accepted my assigned duty for the day, as the recorder in the RMP.

The shift began with the Sr. Officer and me checking out our RMP, making certain that everything was functioning properly. The Sr. Officer was the driver so we took off for our assigned section of the precinct.

As the recorder, usually if there was an arrest during the shift, the recorder would take the arrest, unless the two officers agreed otherwise. That 4x12 shift (generally 4x12 shifts are the busiest shifts) I learned so much from the Sr. Officer.

He knew a lot of the merchants and the people in the community and he was very much respected as he also respected those in the community. I observed his interactions and his people skills and over time I emulated what I learned.

He and I became RMP partners and we worked very well together. My partner was African American and the best patrol partner I ever had. He never disrespected me as woman or female police officer and in the streets he demanded and commanded that the perps that we had to arrest give me the utmost respect. It was truly refreshing working with him as a partner.

After working with my partner for about six (6) months, one of his aspirations in the department did come true. He had applied for and was given recommendations to a specialized unit that he was excited to be part of. With his demeanor and outstanding reputation, there was no way that he could not get the position and he was awarded the position, which was in another precinct division.

I was very happy for my partner but also sad that I was losing such an awesome partner and friend in the precinct. During our RMP patrol days together we never encountered any escalated or derogatory situations that required a Sergeant response. Any situations that appeared to get heated, we were able to utilize our communication skills to de-escalate the situation. That is why I enjoyed working with him as a partner.

We spoke about various police-related incidents, the most recent incident at that time being the shooting of an emotionally disturbed, elderly African American woman in a housing unit in the Bronx.

The elderly woman was shot and killed by an EMS Police Officer who used a 12 gauge shotgun to subdue her after it was alleged that she was acting erratically and charged the Officer with a knife.

There were several rallies that took place in relation to this shooting. I attended one of the Police rallies in civilian clothes and

I was not very happy at some of the insensitive comments that were being made by some officers.

I was not at the scene when this incident took place nor were any of the other officers that were at the rally, but most of the officers were Caucasian and were making statements such as, "she got what she deserved under the circumstances" or I would have done the same thing if I was in that situation."

I won't and can't make any comments one way or the other but I did have many questions. "Was the use of force matrix truly used appropriately in this situation? Could not a second team of trained officers been sent in to de-escalate the situation? What was the rush that the Police had to break into her home at the time when they were already aware that she was very emotionally disturbed? Would the outcome have been the same if it had been an elderly emotionally disturbed Caucasian woman? These are questions that would never be answered. I and my partner had very similar unanswered questions.

After my partner left the precinct we remained friends and are friends to this very day. I had the option of staying in the RMP and acquiring another partner for the sector of the precinct that I patrolled in the RMP.

The new partner assigned to the RMP had seniority over me, so he had the choice of being the driver or the recorder for the day. We began our first shift together on an 8 x 4 shift.

The word in the precinct, especially amongst the African American officers, was not to ride with this officer who was Caucasian, because he always would escalate situations that did not warrant being escalated. He also had a history of using excessive force unnecessarily.

I accepted my assigned duty for the day as the recorder in the RMP. It was a gray, rainy day. As we patrolled the assigned neighborhood my partner was doing quite a bit of talking (more like bragging) about how long he'd been in the precinct, how many arrests he'd made and how many perps he had to "tune-up."

After he finished bragging about himself, he asked me, "So how many arrests have you made and what did you learn from your prior partner? How many perps did we 'tune-up'"? He also inquired if I was aware of the Officer's Code of Silence (as he called it). For the purpose of not wanting the shift to be a long and boring one by me tuning out this hypocrite of a partner, I selectively answered some of his questions and others I chose not to answer. I informed him that my partner had taught me quite a bit and showed me the various areas in the community that were known "Hot Spots."

I educated him that I had only made one arrest since I came out of the academy almost a year prior, and that arrest was made while I was in my NSU. I told him my former partner and I never had to "tune-up" any of the perps that we had transported, because it was not necessary to do so. We used our verbal communications and that worked well for us.

This idiot of an officer then assured me that as long as he and I were going to be partners he was going to show me how to "tune up" a "mouthy perp" as well as some other things I needed to know how to do, like to find a spot to snooze while on duty.

From his conversation, I knew I did not like this officer and as far as I was concerned today would be my first and last day working with him. I answered no more of his questions and did not have much conversation with him.

It was a gray rainy day and my partner appeared to have a high level of anxiety. He blasted the radio in the RMP as if it was his personal car and we did not have the dispatcher radio to listen to for calls or jobs in our section of the community. He was tapping the dashboard very loudly as he was driving, I guess he wanted my attention and he was going to do anything to get it.

I just sat in the passenger seat and was observing what was going on outside in the community verses having to talk with this hypocrite of a partner of mine. I noticed the Sunday Church goers were out early waiting to get into the Churches in the community.

As we were patrolling the area, I noticed my partner began to speed up in the RMP as we drove closer to the sidewalk where there was a group of Church goers standing awaiting entrance into their Church. Adjacent to the side walk, where the people were standing, was a large puddle of water. I was sitting in the passenger seat closest to the curb when I heard my partner laugh out loud, and stating "Watch how these "N" word jump!"

He accelerated and drove through the puddle of muddy water which splashed on several of the people on the side walk.

It all happened so fast. I turned to my partner screaming at him and attempting to steer the steering wheel away from the curb at the same time. "What the hell is wrong with you, you damn fool?"

My partner drove off down the street laughing loudly, finding what he did hilarious. I did not find his actions to be funny, nor did I find his name calling appropriate. I radioed for the Sergeant, to meet with the Police Officer, no emergency, but as soon as possible.

The Sergeant was asking via radio, "What is the condition at the location where the Officers were requesting assistance."

At this point my partner had driven a few blocks down from where he splashed the Church goers and he looked at me stating, "You better respond to the Sergeant's question, with a valid reason for your request to meet with him."

All I could think of to say on the radio was, "Officer will advise upon Sergeant's arrival." I then gave the location where we were parked. I also observed what appeared to be a crowd of people walking in the street towards where we were parked. I turned to my partner and stated, "You need to get us out of here since you started this mess."

My partner drove another few blocks away and around the corner and parked the RMP. I got out of the vehicle and radioed the Sergeant with our new location. I chose to wait outside the vehicle because I was totally livid with this idiot partner's unprofessional acts and his derogatory language.

Once the Sergeant's RMP arrived, I walked over to his vehicle and observed that beside the Sergeant's driver and himself as the passenger, there was a rookie officer sitting in the rear of his vehicle. I requested to speak with the Sergeant one on one. The Sergeant declined the one on one and inquired what the condition was.

I informed the Sergeant of the negative actions of my partner and the damages he caused to some of the Church goers clothing that were waiting to enter church. The Sergeant stated, "I wonder if the crowd of people we passed by who were shouting at our vehicle as we passed were some of the Church people you mentioned?"

The Sergeant stated he wanted to speak to my partner, so the Sergeant got out of the vehicle and walked over to where my partner was parked.

The Sergeant's driver was looking at me in a not so friendly manner and I looked right back at him. The Sergeant spent several moments talking with my partner. He called for the rookie officer that was in the rear of his car to come to the RMP that my partner was driving. The rookie got in the passenger side of the vehicle and they drove off. The Sergeant walked back to where I was standing and he stated, "Well PO Brooks denies that he intentionally splashed anyone on the sidewalk, and he denied that he called anyone the "N" word. It's your word against his. I thought it best that you two no longer drive together as partners so that is why I put the other rookie in the car with him. You officer, are now SP12 (Special Post 12) a foot post."

The Sergeant stated that he was going to drive back in the direction that they came from to see if he observed any of the remaining crowd walking and he would inquire with them about what happened.

The Sergeant's final words to me as he entered his vehicle was, "If anyone should approach you about the alleged incident that took place today, escort them back to the precinct and let them speak with the desk officer." Then the Sergeant and his driver drove off into the sunset. By the way, did I mention that the rookie officer that took my place in the vehicle was Caucasian?

After the incident with my new partner acting foolish, I decided that I would do better walking a foot post in the community, so shortly thereafter I put in a written request for a foot post and the request was granted.

One day while performing my duties as a Foot Post Officer, another officer and I, were re-assigned from our foot posts and directed to escort an EDP (emotionally disturbed person) to the hospital to be treated for some minor self-inflicted injuries and to be assessed for his mental capacity. This was my first encounter in dealing with an EDP.

The other officer and I rode in the ambulance with the EDP, who was being treated in the ambulance for his injuries to his leg. The EDP was handcuffed to the rails of the bed, while in the ambulance. The EDP was very calm the whole time that he was in the ambulance and awaiting to be seen by the doctor. Once exiting the ambulance the EDP was placed in a wheelchair and handcuffed from behind for safety precautions. Once in the ER, triage room the doctor requested that we remove the handcuffs.

We expressed to the doctor the handcuffs were on the EDP for safety precautions, but he demanded that the cuffs be removed in order to assess the EDP's injuries.

My partner removed the handcuffs and within five seconds all hell broke out in that triage area. The EDP unexpectedly kicked my partner in his groin and my partner went down. The EDP went to go for my partner as he was going down, I took out my night stick, striking him numerous times, which apparently he did not feel. I don't know where the doctor disappeared to, but I called a 10-13 over the radio. The EDP, a small, 5'4" man, had phenomenal strength and turned to me and flung me like a rag doll into a metal radiator, which was against the wall. I slammed into the radiator striking my lower back and my head against the wall. I wasn't a little woman, so it took some strength for him to throw me the way he did.

The EDP's eyes were dilated but it did not appear that he was cognizant to what was going on. Several hospital police were now on the scene attempting to subdue the EDP. My partner for the day was still down on the floor lying in a fetal position holding his crotch area.

I was assisted to a standing position by two other Officers who arrived on the scene in minutes. The EDP was finally subdued, but it took about seven (7) hospital and NYPD officers combined to subdue him. I don't know where this EDP got all of his strength from but he was like the Incredible Hulk.

There were so many things going through my mind as this incident was occurring. How much force should be used in this situation? My gun would be inappropriate at this time because there were others in the small triage area. Mace would not be a good tool to use. I decided my night stick or radio was the best option. I was glad that no shots were fired.

The officer who was on the floor and I were taken to triage to be assessed for our injuries. The officer who was kicked in the groin was retained in the hospital for additional testing and observation. I was given a MRI and found to have a herniated disc in my lower back. I was sent home with pain meds and directed to alternate ice packs and heating pads. The next day not only was I bruised, but I could not walk. I had excruciating pain down my legs and in my lower back. I was out of work for a while due to the EDP incident. Ultimately, I healed enough to go back to work but suffered with continual low back pain for years.

Upon my return to duty I went back to foot patrol but was assigned an area that was not far from the precinct. I spent approximately six (6) months as a Community Police Officer and because of my presence out in the street the store merchants and the various agencies hierarchy in the community wrote a letter of recommendation on my behalf to the Mayor of New York.

The letter afforded me an opportunity to transfer from the 73rd Precinct to a specialized unit called the "Recruitment Retention Unit" which was located downtown Manhattan. This was the same unit that the officer who assisted me in getting on the job a few years earlier worked in.

This was truly my Golden Opportunity to make a difference in people lives. Once the transfer took place, I was no longer required to wear a uniform except when I was assigned to "a special detail."

CHAPTER 8

Applicant Processing Division Recruitment / Retention Unit

❧

I began my career as a Recruitment/Retention Officer in September of 1985. The unit consisted mainly of Officers of Color and one male Caucasian Officer.

We also had two Police Administrative Aides and our Sergeants, who also were women of color. Everyone in the unit got along very well and we became a very close unit. We worked diligently to recruit the best of the best from various colleges, high schools and community outreaches to become New York's Finest.

I shadowed behind a few of the Senior Officers for a couple of weeks and learned the protocol of recruiting and retaining candidates to become NYPD's Finest. Recruitment/Retention Unit was just one of the units within the Applicant Procession Division, which had several Investigative Units throughout the boroughs of New York.

I spent eight and a half years and received my Detective Specialist Shield from working within RR/APD units. All of the Officers who worked in the RR Unit, celebrated birthdays, weddings, children's births, anniversaries, and unfortunately, we cried and shared tears through divorces and even deaths of our loved ones. What we had in common was that we all were committed to advocating for those candidates who were considered borderline candidates. Some had been disqualified during the course of their process via a medical, psychological or investigative disqualification.

Don't get me wrong, some of these candidates were disqualified rightfully so. But some, especially persons of color were disqualified because of the power of creative writing or by weeding them out by process of elimination. Allow me to give you a scenario of two candidates both in their early 20s, one resided in Suffolk County, New York and the other resided in Bronx, New York.

One of them automatically qualified, while the other did not. For the purposes of this example I will call the candidates, Candidate # 1 and Candidate #2.

Candidate # 1 qualified medically, psychologically and had no red flags in his background history according to the Investigator who completed the case. Candidate #1 had five DUI's (driving under the influence of Alcohol) from the ages of 18 through 22. He was approximately 23 years old at the time he was processing as a NYPD candidate. He also had some points on his license due to these DUIs.

The Investigator was very coy, cunning, descriptive and creative in writing the Summary Investigation for Candidate #1. The Investigator highlighted that Candidate #1 had done some volunteer work with a politician in his community during his early teen years. The Investigator then stated Candidate #1 engaged in activities with the wrong crowd as a teenager, which led him to his drinking and driving. The Investigator summarized that Candidate #1 has since matured and has not had any DUIs in one year, which reflected a level of growth and maturity, exactly the type of Police Officer that NYPD was looking for.

Now, Candidate #2 passed the medical and psychological but was placed on investigative hold for jumping a turnstile in the Bronx while he was a young teenager. There was no other derogatory history for Candidate #2, who was currently at the approximate age of 24 years old. The Investigator for Candidate #2, wrote the investigative summary very similar to the following: This candidate is not a viable candidate for NYPD Police Academy because although it was some time ago that he received the "C" summons for jumping the turnstile, he showed a flagrant disregard for authority by jumping the turnstile while the Transit Staff was in the token booth, directing candidate to stop, which he failed to do. The candidate was stopped and questioned by the Transit Officer on the platform and was issued a "C" summons for his actions. Candidate #2 did pay a fine for the summons. According to the Investigator, the current concerns were that this Candidate may have a harboring desire to disobey authority and this was not the type of Candidate, that NYPD should have representing them.

After reviewing these two cases, I found it very hard to comprehend how Candidate #1 was a more viable Candidate than Candidate #2, when Candidate #1's investigation had more recent offenses than candidate #2. Plus, Candidate #1 had points on his license, not to mention the many DUI offenses he had.

Candidate #1 was qualified and ready to be appointed to the next upcoming Academy class. Candidate #2 was on investigative hold, and would have missed the next academy class had not the officers from Recruitment/Retention supported and directed the Candidate on what he needed to do to get off investigative hold. Candidate #2 presented his Investigator with several character reference letters. One of the letters was from a Deputy Chief in NYPD who attested to Candidates #2's current character.

Needless to say, Candidate #2 was appointed to the same Academy class as Candidate #1. I did not mention that Candidate #1 was Caucasian and Candidate #2, was Hispanic.

During my tenure as a RR/APD Investigator I met some truly wonderful and committed officers who were dedicated to hiring the best candidates for New York's finest. We did not always see eye to eye, but we agreed to disagree on some situations. There were many civil unrest incidents that occurred during my tenure as Police Officer/Detective Specialist from 1984 through 1994. I was assigned to the special details, where I had to wear my uniform. The rallies that were the result of the civil unrest incidents I attended in either plain clothes, or if assigned to the detail I wore my uniform.

There were multiple rallies after the death of Yusef Hawkins in the Bensonhurst section of Brooklyn, in August 1989. Mr. Hawkins was a 16-year-old African American youth who was in Bensonhurst looking to buy a car and was murdered by a Caucasian perpetrator who was later convicted of 2nd degree murder. Reverend Al Sharpton, held rallies in Bensonhurst daily, which resulted in Reverend Sharpton being seriously injured by knife stabbing. Unfortunately, Yusef Hawkins was the third killing of an African American male by a Caucasian man or men, during the 1980's. (Willie Turks in June of 1982 in Brooklyn and Michael Griffin in December 1986).

There was a lot of racial tension in various communities during this time as well as underlying racial tension within the police department.

(https://en.wikipedia.org/wiki/Death_of_Yusef_Hawkins).

During these rallies, there was always a heavy presence of NYPD officers on the scene for crowd control. For me these rallies were a double-edge sword, especially when present in uniform. Many of the people rallying were people of color who were frustrated by the unnecessary murders of people of color by Caucasian men who apparently had very barbaric ways and no regard for human life.

As an African American female, I could relate to the pain and purpose for the people in the community rallying. But as the African American Female Police Officer assigned to perform crowd control, I was called all types of derogatory names by those rallying. I had a job to perform, which was to keep the peace and crowd control. Some of my fellow officers had the same sentiments as the barbaric men who committed the horrific murders of these three black men. It was a very complicated and difficult time, but I always held fast to the oath that I took, "To Protect and Serve." The question at these rallies was, who was I protecting, myself from the rally goers and my peers, or the rally goers from my peers?

After these special detail assignments were over, I was happy that I was returning to the Retention Unit and not back to patrol. It was a totally different feeling returning to a precinct that consisted of 80% Caucasian officers, verses returning to the Retention/APD Unit that had more officers of color who could relate to the emotions of the rally goers.

On the dates following the rallies we often had discussions in the office to hash out our feelings and vent what we felt when other officers made disparaging remarks or the people in the community made disparaging remarks. Being in both the

Retention and Applicant Processing Units helped me to mature as a Police Officer and as a person. I was able to make a difference in some of the candidate's lives who were initially disqualified for whatever reason, but because of the Officers in the Unit, diligence and assistance, some of these candidates were actually hired as NY's Finest.

CHAPTER 9

The Phone Call

*I*n 1990 my only son was a 13-year-old latch-key child. (A child who is at home without adult supervision for some part of the day, especially after school until a parent returns from work.) Every day he would call in and let me or my peers at work know that he arrived home safely from school and I had my neighbors checking in on him.

One day I received a call from my son, who was out of breath, very upset, excited and was trying to tell me something that happened to him. He was so upset I could not understand all of what he was saying other than someone had called him the "N-word". I was able to calm him down and ascertain where he was and what had happened. My son was home.

As he began to tell me what had happened to him, he was so upset he started crying again. As a mother hearing my son cry over the phone the way he was it alarmed, alerted and upset me and I knew I had to get home to him as soon as I could. My son finally was able to tell me that on his way home from school a police car pulled over to the curb where my son was walking.

The Officer from the passenger side jumped out and grabbed my son by the back of his neck (when I arrived home several hours after the incident my son still had the fingerprint marks in his neck) and stated, "I got you little nigger."

He then mashed my son's face against the back window of the vehicle where an older Caucasian woman was sitting, and he asked her, "Is this the nigger that took your pocketbook?"

The woman told the Officer, "NO" and the officer kept asking the elderly woman "Are you sure that he's not the one?" The officer then continued to hold onto my son's neck and pushed him on the side walk and stated, "Now get out of here Nigger."

As I was hearing what my son was saying to me, I was on my way out the door of my work office. I was enraged, angered and pissed at every Caucasian male cop who had that racist, bigoted attitude and got joy out beating up and killing innocent people. I was very happy that my son was alive to tell what happened to him.

As I continued to listen to my son, he advised that the bodega store owner came out to help him and mentioned he saw everything. The incident happened right in front of the bodega at the curbside. The store owner also attempted to calm my son and informed my son to go home and let his parents know what happened to him. The store owner told my son to have his parents come speak to him about what he saw. That was exactly what I was going to do in my travels home.

My son is and was a very respectful young man, well mannered, known and liked in the culturally diversified community where we lived. Not only was he an academic achiever, he was athletically skilled and played various sports, especially basketball.

As the son of an African American female cop and knowing what I knew from experience or working with some of the patrol officers in the black communities, I made it my business to teach him and some of his friends of all nationalities on how to respond to a police officer via role plays.

My son was taught if ever stopped by an officer to never be aggressive in any manner. He is to have his hands up or out in plain view so it can be seen that he had nothing in his hands. He was taught not to make any sudden movements or gestures. He must address the officers as "Yes Sir, Yes Ma'am" and he is to follow the officer's directives unless those directives could lead to his physical injury.

He was also taught to memorize the name on the officer's name tag and if he could also memorize the shield number that would be in the same area where the name tag was. I also taught him if he could not get the name or shield number, if the officers were riding in a police vehicle, he should memorize the vehicle plate number, and if possible the time of day.

My first stop in route home, I stopped at the bodega store. The owner was familiar with my face because I made many purchases from his store over the years that we lived in the community. I officially introduced myself as the mother of the young man who was stopped by the police in front of his store. The store owner told me that he observed everything that happened to my son.

He did not hear all of the communications, but he did see the officer on the passenger side jump out the car and grab my son (who had just walked past the police vehicle), by the back of his neck, and shoved my son's face into the glass at the back seat window.

The store owner stated he could not clearly see who was in the back seat, but the owner did hear the officer ask, whoever was sitting in the back seat, "Are you sure this isn't him?"

The store owner stated the officer continued to grab my son by the back of his neck as the officer turned my son away from the vehicle still holding his neck, and pushed him down, saying, "Now get out of here Nigger."

I asked the store owner was he sure that was what he heard the officer state, and he said, "yes." The store owner also provided me with the plate number of the police vehicle.

I inquired if the store owner would be willing to repeat what he stated to me if asked by anyone investigating the incident. He stated he had no problem in telling what he saw and heard. He believed in telling the truth and he felt that the officer was very abusive to my son both physically and verbally. He stated my son looked totally terrified at what was happening to him.

The store owner provided me with his contact information and apologized for what my son went through and for whatever I was going to have to go through in my follow up of this incident.

I did not inform the bodega owner that I too was an officer because not only was I offended by this ignorant officer's actions, I felt the anger raging through my body and the thoughts of what happened to me as a child being called, "Coon and Monkey" by Caucasian officers and the feelings of confusion I had as a child.

I had to face my child and admit that I made a mistake in telling him that police officers were in the community to protect him and those in the community. I had to explain to him about good and bad cops and it is not always easy to know the difference.

When I arrived at our apartment my son heard my keys in the door and came running to me. I just held him making sure I was gentle to touch around his neck area. He turned around so I could see the finger print marks in the back of my son's neck. (I'm sure every parent could identify with the rage that continued to surge through my body especially after seeing these prints on my son's neck. Knowing everything my son told me was confirmed by an eye witness).

I had to be calm in the midst of the storm. My son provided me with the plate number of the police vehicle that the officers were driving and the name of the officer that grabbed him by the neck. I informed my son that I was going to follow up with what happened to him and find out what actions we could take about the abuse that he encountered. I asked my son if he could move his head from side to side, which he did.

I asked him if he had any pain and he advised he had a headache. I took my child to the hospital emergency room to be treated for his bruises and his headache. We had our discussion about good cops and bad cops and the reality of there being good and bad people in every walk of life. I apologized to him for what he encountered and began to explain to him what I believed may have happened, never indicating that the officer was correct in the way he handled the situation nor was he correct in his name calling.

I informed him that from what he described happened, apparently, the lady sitting in the rear of the police vehicle was probably robbed by someone, who took her pocketbook.

Depending on the urgency of the crime that was committed the officers would have received a call from the 911 radio dispatcher indicating an alleged crime had taken place or was taking place and the dispatcher would have provided a description of the alleged perp over the radio if the dispatcher had a description.

A second scenario could have been that the woman saw a police car in the area where she was robbed and flagged the officers. They stopped and put her in the car to gather a description of the alleged perp who had robbed her and then put the description over the radio to the 911 dispatcher.

I advised my son that there could be various scenarios as to why and how the woman wound up in the back of the car. The concern for me was did my son match the description that was given to the officers either by the dispatcher or by the victim. In either case the name calling was unprofessional and racially biased and the officer's actions, to grab my son by the back of his neck as he walked past the police car, was physically abusive.

Patrol officers during that time were required to complete a stop and frisk form if they stopped, frisked and detained anyone for any reason and then let them go. Many patrol officers were not completing these forms. My son was treated and released from the emergency room and I was directed to give him over- the-counter pain relievers, which is what I did.

The next day I took off from work to go to the local precinct where the patrol officers worked and I had my son go with me. Upon arrival to the precinct, I had my son sit as I walked over to the desk officer, who was a Lieutenant. Initially I did not identify myself as a police officer because I had my son with me.

I inquired if the officers who had stopped my son were available in the precinct. He stated that they were on patrol and I advised that I wanted to file a complaint against the officer who bruised my son's neck and called my son a racially biased name. The Lieutenant requested that I have a seat. I noticed that there was only one person in the 124 room, (this is the room where most of the paperwork is brought in by the police officers and given to the Police Administrative aides to type. This also was where civilians who would call or walked in to the precinct could make a report or retrieve a report number).

The woman in the 124-room appeared to be the PAA, who was typing the reports. As I sat with my son in the waiting area in the precinct for what seemed to be forever, my son pointed out the police officer who grabbed his neck. As the officer was walking into the precinct, I walked towards him and called out his name. He slightly turned to face me and I asked, "So you like to call children names while bruising them at the same time?" He gave me the look like, who the f--- are you? He kept walking to the back of the precinct.

I knew not to follow him, so I walked back over to the desk officer and asked how much longer it would be before the PAA, would take my complaint. My son and I had been sitting for over an hour. The Lieutenant stated, the staff was getting ready to change shifts and I would have to wait until after they made the change. A short time later, I walked back over to the 124 room and asked the PAA if she was available to take a complaint, which she did. I did identify myself to the PAA as a Police Officer. The PAA provided me with the complaint number and advised that I should follow-up on this complaint. She affirmed that the same two officers who I made the complaint against had numerous previous civilian complaints alleging excessive use of force.

Within a two-week period from when I filed the complaint, I received a call from someone identifying himself as an Internal Affairs Investigator. I met with this IAD Investigator a few times and the outcome of our meetings about the complaint I filed against the officers who abused my son was found to be unsubstantiated or a more appropriate word used, unfounded.

I inquired how or what determined the complaint to be unfounded. The response I received was, "There was not enough evidence to substantiate that the officers, 1) stopped and frisked my son (no stop and frisk report was found in my son's name. That's because the officers never completed one). 2) There was insufficient evidence that the officers used any derogatory or racial name calling or that the officers used abuse of authority.

(I submitted pictures of the fingerprint marks on my son's neck and copies of the ER visit and diagnosis that took place on the same date of the incident.)

I asked the investigator how could that possibly be, when I provided the names of persons who witnessed the incident on the complaint. The Investigator stated all witnesses were contacted and their responses led to the insufficient evidence decision.

I truly did not expect anything less than what I was hearing from this investigator. I am a firm believer that you cannot have any specific unit within any organization to properly investigate any negative allegations objectively and fairly against anyone in the organization that they work for and receive a paycheck from.

Due to this abuse of authority incident by the police upon my son and several months later, my son and several other students were robbed at their Junior High School by an older African American youth with a knife, I made the decision to relocate my son to a private school, in the suburbs of Paoli, PA. As a single mom raising an African American teenage young man in Brooklyn, New York, I had to make a safe haven for my only child. My child was a straight A student in his Junior High School, with not only his academic skills, but he also was very talented athletically. So the all-boys school in Paoli, PA had no problem accepting him along with the tuition check I paid monthly. Paying for my son's education was well worth it.

CHAPTER 10

A Tragedy That Turned Into My Plight

As mentioned in an earlier chapter the police officers within the Retention Unit worked very well together and oftentimes shared many hours together off duty as well. We were a family.

The Retention Unit and several of the Investigation Units relocated from 346 Broadway in Manhattan, to the Old York College Building in Jamaica Queens where we continued to perform the applicant processing for candidates.

One day in the early part of 1991, at the start of our 8x4 shift, as we normally did, someone took the breakfast orders for everyone in the unit and usually two people would go pick up the order.

Trina and I decided we were going to pick up the order once it was called in. As we waited in the unit, we were having a conversation about our children and family life. Trina had two small children, one was about 10 months old and the other was about 2 years old. She was so proud of her children as every mother is. She showed me pictures of her sons as I showed her some pictures of my teenage son in his school in Pennsylvania.

Both of us were proud mothers of very handsome sons. Trina stated that she needed to go downstairs to her locker and would return shortly so that we could go pick up the food order.

Approximately five minutes later I heard what appeared to be the sound of a fire cracker go off somewhere in the building. Everyone who heard the firecracker sound either took cover or went to investigate what the firecracker sound was, with guns in hand. I then heard shouts of "get an ambulance quick, an officer is down in the female locker room."

The hierarchy in the building quickly responded to the basement and no additional officers were allowed in the female locker room. My mind was racing as I tried to make it through the crowd of officers who had gathered on the steps and in the hallways. I heard the sirens outside the building.

Some officers were crying and screaming, "OMG, what happened to Trina?" At that moment, it dawned on me that Trina was the officer that was hurt. I had no idea how severely she was injured or how she got injured. I was not able to get downstairs to be by her side. I was in a daze. Actually, I guess, more of a shock, because I was waiting for Trina to come back upstairs so that we could pick up our food order and to finish our conversation.

Unfortunately, that never happened. Trina was transported to the hospital where she later died. It was alleged that Trina shot herself in the head with her own revolver. After learning of how Trina died nothing made sense to me. There were no signs, at least not what I observed, while we were sharing our motherhood experiences and pictures, that she was depressed.

I replay those moments repeatedly in my mind on what I could have done differently, even to this day. I went to trauma counseling after Trina's death. I was told by the therapist that there really was nothing I could have done differently, especially if Trina had not displayed any signs of depression.

I felt that there was something that I could do. There was a collection that was taken up in the unit for Trina's family and of course I contributed, but I still felt like I needed to do more.

I began to research statistics about police officers who committed suicide and I learned that it was difficult retrieving information on police suicides because it was a very sensitive and embarrassing situation for the families of the deceased officers. The subject of suicide was viewed by many officers as something that was "taboo." For an officer to admit that they were fearful or depressed was considered "weak." (www.nytimes.com, "Police suicide is delicate topic of film", by George James, Published: October 10th, 1991)

During my plight to learn about the suicides, I learned from a female police officer peer who advised that she was working with another officer collaborating with some of the family members of police officers who had committed suicide.

My female co-worker, Dawn, and I met with the officer who was in communications with the families of some of the deceased officers. During our meeting, Officer Franks expressed his goal and mission was to be proactive in helping police officers who showed signs of depression but would not seek help within the Department.

These officers feared being ridiculed, ostracized and having their guns removed for seeking help within the Police Department. During this meeting and several additional meetings thereafter,

Officer Franks, Dawn and myself, researched how to become a "Not for profit" organization that could assist both the Police Officers and families in their needs for psychological assistance outside of the Police Department.

It is alleged, that from "1986 through 1990, 34 NY City police officers killed themselves, (per statistics provided by the police.) www.nytimes.com, "police suicide is delicate topic of film", by George James, published: October 10th, 1991). These statistics did not include the death of Trina. Officer Franks, Dawn and I, agreed that we would not consult, promote or discuss our desires to assist our deceased or depressed officers and their families unless we were doing it on our own time. One of the wives of a fallen officer, who had taken his life was very vocal, viable and a key source in getting our plight publicized and she was working towards getting media publicity.

We assisted Marie, the fallen officer's wife, who had now stepped up to be the spokesperson of "The Fallen Officer Chapter."

We gathered NYPD officer suicides information and resources from wherever we could find the story. We met with the families of some of the fallen officers to ascertain if they wanted to share their story of who their love one was and what may have led the officer to his or her depressed state or demise.

Due to Officer Franks, Dawn, Marie and my own efforts and perseverance, Marie was successful via media publicity to schedule a City Hall Hearing in the fall of 1991 to include some of the Mayoral Office personnel and the hierarchy from NYPD to review the concerns and statistics of NYPD's Officer suicides.

As Police Officers when on duty, we were not allowed to speak with the media, so we were present in civilian clothes and each one of us had taken a personal day off to attend the city hall meeting.

During the City Hall meeting, to our surprise Marie presented a documentary called, "By Their Own Hand: Police Suicide."

This was a very powerful video that I know touched my heart. After the video presentation, there was a question and answer session. Many of the questions were geared to the hierarchy of NYPD, which appeared they (the hierarchy) did not have the specific answers to the questions asked and they advised they would have to research the answers.

One specific question that was asked and answered by the hierarchy was: "What is the NYPD going to do to assist in resolving the high rate of suicide within the agency?"

The answer provided was to show this documentary as a training video to all of the officers in the department.

Next step was to create a suicide prevention unit with trained staff to address the needs of our depressed and stressed officers. It was stated that research would be conducted to verify if this unit could use discretion and anonymity when assisting these officers in need. The City Hall meeting ended.

My peers, as well as Marie and I were satisfied with the outcome of this meeting. Exposure about the very limited resources for the officers and their families who needed assistance as well as upcoming training and a new unit to be implemented was the outcome.

Our mission was accomplished although we were not identified as having any direct impact or involvement with the scheduling of this City Hall meeting. At least that's what we thought.

Shortly after the City Hall meeting, I was placed on "Modified Assignment", had my weapons removed and was transferred from my specialized detail at the Applicant Processing Division, where I was promoted to Detective Specialist 3rd grade, for my six years of service in that unit. I was promoted in September 1991 and then transferred to the Psych Services and Medical Unit as modified during the winter holiday season in 1991.

The title as "Modified Assignment" was a stigma within the department.

In these units, I was trained to do what officers called "push or shuffle papers." The reason I was told that I was placed on modified assignment was because of an old line of duty injury I sustained to my back in the mid-1980s, when I was injured by an emotional disturbed person. It was stated that I had taken several sick days over the years because of this injury. To my recollection, I had not taken any recent sick days in regard to this injury.

At some point in the past I had applied for three quarter disability (Line of Duty injury disability) and was denied. This transfer was very disheartening to me because I was removed from a Unit where I had spent more than half of my policing career in. I did not see this transfer as a promotion but rather as a demotion.

Over the next few months and into the New Year, I continued to communicate with Officer Franks and Dawn and learned that they too had been placed on "Modified Assignment," and had their weapons removed as well, shortly after I did.

Because each of us faced the same circumstance of being placed on modified assignment after the City Hall Meeting, we were led to believe that somehow, we were identified as having taken part in the scheduling of the City Hall meeting. Apparently, we must have stepped on some hierarchy's toes or the hierarchy felt that they were embarrassed at the meeting. But something did happen that was related to us helping our fallen officers that led us all to be on modified assignment.

We contacted Marie and informed her of our current situations and we all felt that we should bifurcate our ties now assisting in the "Fallen Officer Group." Marie thanked us for all of our assistance. Officer Franks, Dawn and I did not regret our participation in the "Fallen Officer Group." Especially when it appeared that it resulted in a positive outcome for future officers who may have some depression and may need assistance. At no time that I assisted with this group's mission, which was to assist in getting help for depressed or distressed officers and their families, did I knowingly do anything that was against NYPD's policy.

My peers and I felt it was best if we discontinued our communications with each other since we were apparently being scrutinized. We said our goodbyes and our communications ceased.

I remained on "Modified Assignment" for approximately two and a half years until 1994. I made the best of those years. I met new people, but none that I befriended. I understood that I could not be promoted to any other position as long as I was on "Modified Assignment."

After the first year of being on "Modified Assignment" I did reapply for line of duty disability and was denied a second time. After that denial, I hired an attorney to assist me with getting off "Modified Assignment" and placed back on regular duty, which was a task and was costing me quite a bit of money to retain an attorney.

Prior to this long term "Modified Assignment" status, I had no prior disciplinary actions or derogatory history or documents in my records. Quite the contrary, I had several letters of recommendations from people and store owners in the community where I did my patrol. These letters of recommendations were what led me to be transferred from patrol to the specialized Recruitment and Retention Unit.

CHAPTER 11

The Final Chapter

After spending two years between the medical and psych unit of NYPD in Lefrak City Queens, NY, in February 1994, I reflected on what I was currently doing and where I wanted to be by the end of the year.

I could no longer afford to retain an attorney to assist with me being placed back on regular duty. The questions were, where would I be if I were approved and returned to regular duty? Would I be placed back on patrol or in a Detective Unit, since my current title was Detective Specialist? What will I do or could I do if I continued to remain on "Modified Assignment" indefinitely?

I had no idea and no answers to those questions. I did not see a future for myself within the department anymore since I was being retained on "Modified Assignment." I was into my eleventh year in NYPD and still had nine years to go before retirement. These last two years had been a true travesty of being one of New York's Finest. Waking up and going to work was no longer pleasurable.

It became more of a weight-bearing task that I did not want to deal with anymore, but I had to. I had not made any new associates while working in Lefrak City. Most of my peers working there were "Modified Assignment" also. Everyone had their own little clicks that I did not get myself involved with. Because I did not volunteer to share my business with anyone, I learned that I was given the nickname of "Ms. Anti-Social."

I was never disrespectful to anyone and greeted everyone that I encountered while at work.

My police officer friends and associates I had made through the years seldom had the opportunity to see or spend time with each other anymore. During the few times that I did go out with them after work, someone would make a joke about me "pushing papers" for so long.

Then the question would be asked, "How long are you going to hide in that 'Modified Assignment' status? When are you going to get your weapons back?"

This status that I was labeled as made me feel very insecure, ashamed and ostracized. I never asked to be placed in this status. I was never given a legitimate reason for being in this status for as long as I remained so. I had no clue as to when I would return to full duty.

What I do know is the purpose behind why I believe officer Franks, Dawn and I were placed on "Modified Assignment," was well worth the cause.

If I helped to save a distressed officer from hurting himself, herself or someone else, then I did not mind remaining "Modified Assignment" for as long as it took. I never expressed to any of my police associates about what I did in the "Fallen Officer Group." That was confidential and I knew that some of my peers did not know what confidential meant. Confidential to some of my peers meant telling the world. I did not feel that I owed them any kind of explanation now.

I did not have many civilian friends. But the few that I did have were my true support system during this complicated period of my life. My number one love of my life, my son was now in his senior year of high school in his college prep school in Paoli, PA.

So, I had plenty time to spend by myself after work, since my son was out of state and my husband had recently relocated to Florida.

I became a newly-wed as of August 26, 1993. My husband's employer offered him a lucrative salary increase to relocate his family to Citra, FL by January 1994. We discussed our options and decided that my husband would relocate to Florida in the New Year and we would visit each other as often as we could during the year. The plan was that I would work with NYPD up until my fifteenth year, where I could vest out and pay into my pension until my twentieth year.

The first several months not having my husband present at home and the stressors of feeling non-productive at work due to my "Modified Assignment" began to take a toll on me.

I found an after-work stress reliever. I hired a personal trainer who got me back on the physical, mental and emotional fitness track. Several months passed and I was getting physically and mentally stronger day by day.

I had a different perspective on how I viewed negative situations that I encountered in my life. Instead of viewing my "Modified Assignment" status as a punishment, (which I originally believed it to be since I was retained in that status, without any legitimate reason given for so long) I began to view it as a window of opportunity.

In the summer of 1994 I began to search for employment in the State of Florida realizing that the "Modified Assignment" status may very well be my status quo for the duration of my tenure as a NYPD Police Officer.

I shifted my thoughts and energy to seeing myself residing with my husband in Florida. I began to diligently pursue my career options in North Central Florida where my husband lived.

During my search for employment I learned that the police municipalities in North Florida did not accept lateral transfers from out of state Police Departments and the salary was well below what I was used to making. I also had concerns on how my "Modified Assignment" status would affect my opportunities for employment in Florida.

My prayers were finally answered and I was returned to "Full Duty," with NYPD, in the fall of 1994. I was not immediately re-assigned and remained at Lefrak City bouncing back and forth between the Medical and Psych Units, doing the same thing I did when I was modified.

My full duty return status was posted in the NYPD orders, just as everyone else, whose titles were changed from one title to another, and many of the 27,000 plus officers had access to read these orders.

I had no idea that my status change would create a problem. Apparently, there were several persons (I am uncertain of who they were, or their ranks) had concerns about me now being a "Full Duty" Detective working in the capacity of a "Modified Assignment" Detective.

I did not understand why I was being scrutinized the way that I was, and I did not like the notoriety. My focus now was to find a job in Florida and let NYPD Detective/Police Officer, be a blast from the past.

Sometime during the Holiday season (Thanksgiving through Christmas 1994), I received an acceptance letter from the State of Florida, Department of Corrections to begin an on-the-job training in March of 1995 as a Correctional Officer. I was very ecstatic to have received the offer, although it was several months away.

It did not take much thought or consideration for me to decide to resign as a NYPD Officer after eleven and a half years of service. I was now truly ashamed of being identified as one of New York's finest. During my tenure as a Police Officer/Detective, there were some good times, great things that I learned and some wonderful people that I met.

There were also many horrific and racially-biased situations that I observed from both my peers and from some people in the community for which I took an oath to serve and protect.

Over the years that I served there was a rise of Police brutality and excessive use of force, used against people of color. (www.refworld.org > refworld/*Police Brutality*, publication date, June 1, 1996). From 1983 through 1994 the death toll continued to rise of unarmed people of color being shot by police officers. (m.huffpost.com *The NYPD Has a Long History of Killing Unarmed Black Men*, publication date 07/18/2014).

Although the circumstance presented to the Grand Jury and DA's office, showed some evidence of police wrong doing, the officers never seemed to be convicted. I believe that this was a direct result of the "Blue Wall of Silence or the Code of Silence," where police officers, whether good or bad would not make any statements about any officer's wrong doings they may have observed.

In 1992, and 1994, there were documented incidents where officers of color had been shot by Caucasian officers.

www.refworld.org: refworld/*Police Brutality*...publication date, June 1, 1996).

I had personal interactions with my peers and their behaviors or lack of professional behaviors, and my complaints to the hierarchy of the abuse of authority by some my peers were listed as unfounded, or the behaviors were condoned, (as mentioned earlier in this memoir).

As a patrol officer I was penalized for doing my job (writing summonses to vehicles that were in violation of the Vehicle Traffic Law) in a certain section of Brooklyn where a specific ethnic group resided and then commended for doing the same job in a different section of Brooklyn that had a different ethnic group.

After being what I believed to be anonymous in getting some of the "Fallen Officers" (officers who committed suicide or attempted suicide and their family's) assistance and then being placed on long term, "Modified Assignment" without a legitimate reason, all were enough reasons for me to now depart from NYPD, without further regrets.

I finalized my resignation with NYPD, put in my two weeks' notice, effective 12/22/1994, applied for my pension monies, and notified my husband to contact his company that I would be relocating to Florida to be with him by 12/31/1994. (My husband's company paid for the relocation).

I said my goodbyes to my true friends that I met while being an Officer, my New York family and my civilian friends. I headed out for my new life and new adventures in Florida with my husband.

One chapter of my life closed and the next chapter to begin...

Ravens Memoirs

CHAPTER 1

The Morgue /
Missing Persons Squad

The poor elderly man, died in his apartment and there I was sitting in his living room as he lay on the floor stiff as a board. I was assigned to watch over his body and possessions while I waited for the morgue wagon to come and transport him to the morgue for an autopsy.

You see, that's the procedure in place when a dead person is discovered under suspicious or unknown circumstances. The body is taken to the morgue where an autopsy would be performed to rule out homicide, accident or suicide. The body would then be identified, if possible, and released to family for burial or cremation. I ended up waiting all night long, taking mini naps on his couch (his apartment was quite neat) for the morgue wagon to arrive. You might find this disgusting or even morbid, but when it's 4:00 am and you're exhausted, trust me, you'll fall asleep wherever.

Obviously dead people didn't spook me at all and my interest piqued as I wondered how I could be transferred to the medical examiner's office. It seemed quite interesting to me, after all I did spend the evening with a corpse. The morgue technicians finally arrived at 7:30 the next morning and I returned to the station house, signed out and went home all the while thinking how long it would take for my transfer to go through.

A few weeks later I decided to call the morgue and ask if there were any vacancies and the Morgue supervisor Sergeant Muller offered to interview me. It just so happened that I had to make a visit to the morgue on a homicide and Sergeant Muller asked if I wouldn't mind showing him my fingerprinting technique. He walked me into one of the morgue freezers which contained around 40 bodies. I then went out to the office and retrieved a fingerprint card, and proceeded to grab the cadaver's fingers and begin the process. Before I imprinted the cadavers' inked finger onto the card, the Sergeant stopped me and stated how most cops didn't even make it to that point without getting nauseated. It was no big deal for me, I didn't get dizzy or sick. Sergeant Muller was quite impressed with my performance and assured me that I would be transferred to his team. Actually it was quite exciting and I wanted to do more and find out how the Medical Examiner's office processed their work.

Since I understood that getting transferred to any unit was a lengthy process, I waited patiently. Transfers could take years and oftentimes it would depend on who you knew. Many cops wanted to get transferred to the morgue because the hours were decent with weekends off but the work is grueling, nasty and very smelly. Let me also mention that one had to wear protective outerwear to protect against blood or other body fluids. Since bodies are discovered anywhere, one had to decrease the risk of exposure to all sorts of debris and bacteria.

At that time there were educational requirements if one was to be considered for transfer to the ME's office. One of the educational requirements for the role was a background in nursing or medicine. I decided to pursue my childhood dream of becoming a nurse as I knew this would serve me well after retirement. I enrolled in a community college while awaiting my transfer and two years later earned my associate degree followed by my successful passing of the New York State nursing board exam.

In October 1996, after waiting nearly two years my transfer came through and I couldn't move fast enough. I was thrilled at the opportunity and I was assigned to the Chief Medical Examiner's Office which is located on the northeast corner of 33rd Street in Manhattan. The Medical Examiner's Squad is part of the Missing Persons Unit. I was looking forward to working with detectives from various precincts in the city as they investigated suspicious death cases. I was super excited about starting a new chapter in my life as a detective in the morgue and hopefully my last stop before retirement. With 14 years under my belt I was ready to learn as much as I could about homicides, suicides and other causes of death.

My excitement quickly dwindled when I realized that my presence was not as I had anticipated. My white male co-workers made little effort at welcoming me as part of the morgue team, except for one detective who was very quiet, soft spoken and kept to himself most of the time. The office was very small with room enough for four desks and one small but deep closet where volumes containing hundreds of photos of unclaimed, unidentified decedents were kept. I worked the day shift with Sundays and Mondays as RDOs (regular days off).

Here is where my nursing degree began to pay off as it facilitated my role by providing clear and succinct communication with the physicians performing autopsies. I would then translate the doctor's findings to the detectives assigned to those cases by using police language.

The guys and I served as the liaisons and cases were expeditiously closed or escalated to the precinct detective squad for further investigation if warranted. Our roles were essential as we assisted in solving many deaths by simplifying communication between the medical examiner's office and the police department. This task would not be possible to accomplish without having the appropriate nursing or medical education.

At the time, there was only one female assigned to the chief medical examiner's office in Queens and I had very little contact with her. I noticed that whenever the guys spoke to her on the phone, they were polite. I wondered if they were nice because they knew her or because she was also Caucasian. I wondered if she was ever treated the way I was or did she choose to stay as far away from them as possible to avoid them. I found out later, that she was married to a high ranking officer. I thought perhaps that shielded her from the toxic behaviors of the guys.

The guys in the Manhattan office intimidated me to the point that I wanted to transfer to headquarters and work in the missing persons unit. I felt trapped and fearful. I decided I would reach out to an inspector whom I knew back when I worked at the Applicant Processing Unit located in the 49th Precinct in the Bronx.

A week later I received a call from Luis, who agreed to meet with me and discuss the matter further over dinner. Of course, I agreed. I thought because Luis was a high ranking officer he would be able to at least give me some guidance as to what steps I would need to take. I did not want to get anyone in trouble, but at the same time I didn't want to be subjected to that type of behavior any further. I knew the guys did not want me there, and I wanted the police department to take some type of action. I wanted those cops to be held accountable for their behavior.

Well to no avail, Luis listened and the only thing he suggested is that I wear a wire, record everything and bring it to internal affairs. I did not want the guys to get suspended or lose their jobs. I thought about their families and felt sympathy, so I decided not to wear a wire. Instead, I asked Luis to arrange a transfer for me back to missing persons unit. Luis informed me that this was my only option if I did not want to escalate the matter to internal affairs.

At the ME's office, there were a wide variety of cases, from new mothers sleeping with their infants, accidentally rolling over them and smothering them to death, people committing suicide by jumping out of windows, off rooftops, onto train tracks or self-inflicted gunshot wounds to homicides and motor vehicle accidents.

I continued to learn my role and tried to enjoy it, but at the same time I loathed working with those nasty detectives. They were rude, inconsiderate and did not respect that I too was a detective, nonetheless, I felt intimidated by their behavior.

I quickly determined that they were exaggerating their actions in an attempt to get rid of me. "I simply must tell somebody, and get the hell out of here, get transferred to the Bronx and be in a more comfortable environment," I thought to myself. I was too scared to tell anyone because I knew very well that this job did not have my back. I'd seen it all too often with other female cops who had encountered a hostile work environment. No one wanted to hear about it, much less do anything about it.

Freaking assholes in the New York City Police Department! You just never know the type of people you work with until you work beside them 40-plus hours a week. I had wanted to work in the morgue for years, and this is what I had to deal with.

First of all, I didn't know how and I wasn't sure I was going to get any help especially from any of my supervisors or coworkers. There were many cops going through the same thing, yet I was sure no one wanted to complain about it. The typical response from the supervisors was always, "No one forced you to take this job."

In other words, you were expected to suck it up and tolerate the various insensitive behaviors and negative, sexist attitudes. I felt as though I had to prove that I was "one of the guys" and could take it. That's what a team player did. Surely you would develop a tough skin and, after a while all of that crap would no longer bother you. I didn't buy that. I felt helpless and vulnerable and wanted out.

There was a very narrow spiral staircase that led to the autopsy room from the detective's office. One day my Sergeant asked me to come downstairs to observe an autopsy on a fresh case. As I descended down the stairs he commented to me, "What's the matter Raven, you afraid I might look up your dress?" What the freak was that comment about? I found that statement very offensive, but decided not to say anything. Still, I had an uneasy feeling, but chose to let it go and chalk it up to stupidity. That feeling of uneasiness stayed with me for the rest of the day, "not good" I thought to myself.

I thought of how the Sergeant was probably accountable since he allowed such negative and condescending behavior, but it was hard to prove since he only visited our office about twice a week. It was his responsibility to check up on us making sure we were doing our jobs, and not goofing off. I suspect that since his relationship with the guys was established, he was not aware of their actions, simply because no one, including me, said anything to him.

Being new to the unit, I did not want to complain or start anything, especially if I intended to remain working there. It did however, become gut wrenching and difficult to come to work every day. Maybe, they thought that behavior was ok or not offensive because, again, they were used to it and no females had worked there in a while.

But truly, what would they do if their wives or daughters encountered the same problem in their own jobs? How would they handle it? There was no sensitivity expressed at all. Instead, the guys viewed my presence there as an intrusion. Maybe they thought I was sent there to spy on them and report back to internal affairs, the unit feared by most cops causing them to   experience a little paranoia every now and then. Whatever the reason, I had to devise a plan to get myself transferred out, or take some other course of action.

Sexual harassment was alive and well in the police department. In the mid-1980s incidences involving sexual harassment were not that well defined and police officers had very little to no training about the topic. However, we knew it was happening, and many times those situations were kept quiet, out of the press. Some of the female officers involved, would see no other way out or had very little support, faced with so much pressure, they were left with no choice but to resign.

Every now and then we would hear of some female officer involved in a sexual harassment case involving some high ranking official, but that's as far as it would go with very little information getting back to patrol officers. Therefore, we would forget about it and not even inquire as to the outcome until we read it in the newspapers. Sometimes certain situations would get the attention of the press, but no one really cared. I dare say that it's probably still the culture of the police department today...that of ignoring situations unless the public insisted or the press picked up on it.

One day I decided to conduct my own audio surveillance and bought myself a small recorder, taped it to the underside of my desk, turned it on and left to go home. The next day I listened to the recording and while it was not totally audible, I was able to make out some of what one of the guys was saying. By the way, he was the oldest one in the group and was getting ready to retire in about a year. I heard him say that he did not like my presence there and that for all he knew I was sent there to spy on them. I wondered why he made that comment and thought to myself that if they were conducting their job correctly then there was nothing to be afraid of.

What else could these guys do to make it more difficult for me to do my job? As if their risqué behavior wasn't enough, one day one of the guys made a comment that sent chills down my spine. He commented that he was going to go home and put his "hood on." Of course what else would I think immediately after he made that comment, the KKK!

I wondered if he was an active member of the KKK or was he just bullshitting his way to get acceptance from the other guys.

On a daily basis they would grab their crotches right in front of me and not even think about apologizing to me. I suspected they felt they didn't need to. It was thoroughly disgusting just being in that office with them. What annoyed me even more was the fact that one of the four detectives who sat at his desk next to me never spoke up one way or the other. Tony was a physician's assistant, and I thought he had a very professional demeanor for a cop. However, I felt disappointed in him because as a medical professional, I had expected him to show some compassion for me and advocate in some way or another. It appeared to me, that he did not or could not involve himself, and so he remained as neutral as possible by not interacting with them except when it involved discussing work related issues. The guys respected him or his profession. I'm not sure which one.

As time passed by, I lost all respect for Tony and had very little to say to him. He knew that the guys were behaving inappropriately, but basically didn't have the balls to call them out on their behavior. He silently took the laissez-faire approach, or just didn't care at all.

This reminded me of the lack of cultural sensitivity that the police department demonstrated. Sure, the department hired females and people of color to comply with affirmative action laws, but that was the extent of the cultural awareness. You see, as a cop one had to assimilate into the police department culture, but it was a one-way street. No one forces you to become a cop and the department was not a flexible organization. It did not have to conform to anyone or any group. I managed to deal with the guy's behavior by attempting to engage Tony in conversation and discussing topics unfamiliar to the assholes I was working with. Basically, I used Tony as a buffer to help ease my angst.

The guys never bothered to orient me to my role in the morgue, but sometimes Tony would take the lead and assist me. I thought at times he took pity on me, and that's why he would help me with some of my tasks.

We were all law enforcement officers, but there was no equality among the guys and myself; they made sure of that. The line of demarcation was clearly drawn. Nevertheless, I was going to try and find a way to discover and maintain my happy place, mentally speaking. I wanted to do my job and do it well, but every day I experienced a gut wrenching feeling that made me want to quit the police department all together. The conversations that went on inside that office with no regard for gender, race, or culture was nauseating.

I thought about the possibility that these guys were scarred from their experiences out in the street, coupled with their upbringing. Knowing what I did about them, just the thought of those guys working out in the street and dealing with the public made my skin crawl. They thought they were careful, but every now and again they would slip and say derogatory things about certain cultures, everything from afro-centric hairstyles to facial features of other non-white groups.

They would make fun of people with foreign accents, criticize the poor, and verbally assault the police department for hiring non-whites. All of this was said without regard to me, or my Hispanic origin. I often thought about how ignorant, stupid and narrow-minded these jerks were. That was the world they lived in, and they fed off each other's opinions. I tried very hard to excuse their ignorance, but frankly, I was too disgusted and disappointed to show any compassion for these guys.

The three of them acted in concert all of the time, almost feeding off of each other. Our office door was kept closed most of the time providing a shield of obscurity as they carried on with their lewd behavior. They would go to lunch together but before leaving would not ask if I wanted anything. At first that bothered me but I quickly got used to it and it was no longer an issue for me.

The hostility came in the form of the constant grabbing of their genitals and saying things like "suck this" and making motions as if they were masturbating. That behavior occurred on a daily basis and directly in front of me. I would turn my face but I could tell with my peripheral vision what they were doing.

Their conversations consisted of discussions regarding the vagina and penis, prostitution and people they didn't like within the department.

I thought these guys were too dangerous to be sent out to the streets. Certainly public safety would not be their priority. They were filled with bitterness and hate and their perspectives fueled one another as they continued their toxic behavior. They did not hide the fact that they were very upset that women and other minority groups were joining the ranks of the police department. I believe the police department condoned this type of behavior, by not addressing it among its members. If you permit it, you promote it, is how I felt and thought.

The few females that were assigned to the other borough morgues were of little to no help. They would shrug their shoulders, ignoring the behavior as if to say, "oh well, suck it up".

Then along came Anna. "Cool!" I thought to myself, "Now I have company." She worked alongside me in the morgue over at the Manhattan office. I saw her as a double-edged sword. When it was convenient for her, she would pull out the old "oh well I just work here" card. Other times, she would be as consoling as any other woman. I didn't trust her. She entertained the guy's attitudes and basically really didn't care. I was misguided in my thinking that we were sisters in blue, especially with her being Hispanic, like myself. It took a couple of years for me to find out that she was just as selfish and self-centered as our male counterparts. I guess she wanted to be accepted and considered one of the guys. Her father was a retired sergeant and had suffered a heart attack years prior, forcing him to end his career. The problem was that she was Hispanic, but still tried really hard in her attempt to gain clout with them. Some of the guys knew her dad, but most didn't, and yet I noted how she did gain some level of respect because of that. Anna played the game well. I wondered if she too felt intimidated and, in an effort to shield herself, played along with the guys by laughing at their risqué jokes and ignoring their inappropriate behavior. Not once did she indicate to me that their behavior was bothersome to her. I think she accepted it as normal male bonding behavior, and didn't have much to say about it.

While I thought I had cultivated a friendship with Anna, since we were both assigned to the medical examiner's office, I thought we had a bond between us. After some time I noticed that she would go out to lunch with the guys, and I asked her if she felt at all disrespected by them. She stated that it didn't bother her. I quickly concluded that she was accepting their behavior and did not want to make an issue of it. I think the pressure is too much, and women deal with it by ignoring offensive behaviors to the point of acceptance.

Police officers are a product of their communities. Police departments are not the military, so in essence what you see and hear is what you get. Angry, spiteful, abusive, overbearing, racist, narcissistic people make up many police departments. Kindness and patience are virtues that one is taught from a very young age and can quickly disappear, if the individual is unable to cope with all of the stressors that law enforcement comes with. I view those stressors as hazards of the job. You see, not everyone is exposed to those stressors, and having to deal with them on a daily basis can be overwhelming. I've been taught, like others, from a very young age that kindness goes a long way. Some however, forget that as they go through life dealing with adversity.

My co-workers were disgusting, insensitive, burnt out, desperate, rude, and totally unaware of how toxic they made the work environment.

Nevertheless, I did my best to cope and as time passed, things changed, thankfully for the better. Gradually, one by one the guys retired, and I was sent back to the morgue in Manhattan where I remained until my twentieth anniversary.

With the aftermath of 9/11, officers from different precincts were sent to the morgue to assist with the identification of the remains. They were also assigned other duties, such as, cleaning up the site at Ground Zero, transporting other officers to different areas, as well as other tasks assigned to them by their superiors. It wasn't too long after 9/11 that I decided it was time to retire and pursue nursing.

CHAPTER 2

Applicant Investigations Unit

In 1986, I was transferred to the Applicant Investigations Unit which is responsible for the processing of potential police department candidates. One investigation can take almost two years to complete and an Investigator can have up to as many as 80 cases.

Applicant Investigations was a decent place to work, however, it too had its share of politics and gossip. One of the things I admired about working in that unit is if you were not a match, then you were transferred to another unit. There was much work to be done and if you could not carry your weight, you were immediately transferred out.

The police officers conducting the candidate's investigations had to deal with heavy caseloads, as well as timelines placed by supervisors to close out or complete two cases per month. A task not so easy to accomplish, since much of the paperwork had to be provided by the candidates interested in becoming police officers. It proved to be a time consuming task. Candidates were asked to provide their Investigators (our titles) with employment, criminal and educational background information in order to compile into a chronological format their cases, and submit them for approval prior to making a decision.

Only qualified candidates would be sworn in as officers, once they had passed the criminal background check as well as their physical and psychiatric exams. Once hired, the recruit is placed on probation for one entire year and could be fired for any reason prior to the end of their probationary period.

Some lifelong friendships developed while working in that unit. Romantic relationships also bloomed, since we all worked in close proximity with one another. There were even marriage proposals that unfortunately ended in divorce, which proved an even more interesting workplace due to all of the drama that occurred. I found it rather amusing and entertaining. I felt good working there, but after about six years I wanted to go somewhere else, and do something more meaningful.

We were a team of culturally diverse officers, with similar interests and for the most part, everyone got along well. Work became routine, boring and definitely not intellectually stimulating. My Lieutenant got wind of my interest to apply to the morgue and offered assistance, by allowing me to work different shifts so that I could obtain my nursing degree. He told me that he too was going back to school, and understood the pressures associated with both work and school. To this day, I am extremely grateful for his support of my dream and vision.

In early 1991, to our surprise, we were informed that members of any investigative unit had the opportunity to earn a merit promotion. We were each interviewed and promoted to Detective

3rd grade, the lowest of three grades. As a single parent, that signaled good news for me as it meant a significant increase in my salary. That also meant transfers were impending, and I had already positioned myself for a possible transfer to the morgue, so I knew I was headed in the right direction.

My promotion ceremony took place in 1992 at Police Headquarters located at One Police Plaza, in Lower Manhattan. It was pretty cool, and I really felt like a valuable member of the police department. Not long afterwards, most of my fellow detectives began getting transferred to different detective squads such as robbery, burglary, homicide, or sex crimes units and I was transferred to the Missing Persons Squad, which was part of the Medical Examiner's Unit or Morgue.

I was curious, and felt really good that I was going to be helping people find their loved ones, dead or alive.

CHAPTER 3

Orchard Beach Detail

While working at the 46th Precinct, I received a phone call from a Lieutenant who asked me if I was interested in working at the beach, patrolling the front gate keeping unwanted people out of the beach during the night. He informed me that it would be a midnight shift from 7:00pm to 7:00am. I accepted, and began my shift the summer of 1983. I saw it as an opportunity to leave the mean streets of the Bronx, and work my way into an investigative unit.

I must admit, sitting in a patrol car alone, from dusk to dawn was boring, and frankly there were many times when I would take some cat naps. I sat by a barrier had to be manually opened and closed. Off duty cops would come by with friends and of course, I would let them in. One night a slew of cops and supervisors identified themselves to me by showing me their shields and ID cards and I let them in. They would "tin" me which means to show me their shields, and they had easy entry with no questions asked. One night, apparently there was a party going on, but since I had to guard the gate, I couldn't ascertain how many cops went through or what kind of party it was.

I did find out later that day, that there had been a swimming pool installed on the roof of the police substation. From what I also heard, quite a few officers ended up in trouble for using the pool during work hours and the commanding officer of the beach detail was reassigned. The pool situation became a joke, and tee shirts were made depicting cops with their uniform hats, shirtless diving into a pool. It was party city until they got busted and it was all over the newspapers. Big bosses got transferred, some cops got disciplined by getting transferred, and it all ended.

Still, I thought that summer was pretty cool for me, since I didn't have to deal with criminals, traffic tickets or court appearances. I guess I felt like I needed a break from patrol and all of the nonsense and negativity. After the beaches were officially closed. It wasn't too long after, I returned to the hell-house, 'the 46th Precinct', that I transferred out from.

CHAPTER 4

46th Precinct

In 1983 I was assigned to the 46th Precinct in the central part of the West Bronx. This precinct was coined the "Alamo," back in the 1970s. The neighborhood surrounding the 46th was bustling with homicides, robberies, and burglaries during late night hours. The neighborhoods consisted of an economically disadvantaged population, trying to make it day by day. Almost every corner had a "bodega" or neighborhood grocery store which charged higher prices than supermarkets, but provided convenience for residents to shop for their staple items.

The 46th was considered a very busy precinct, and that it was. Officers were always bringing in an arrest or handling a domestic dispute. I have to admit that even though I grew up in a modest apartment and was blessed to have both parents, I was taken aback by how some people lived. I was required to work day and evening shifts with one midnight shift in between, and the things I observed frightened me when I first started working there. After some time, I became desensitized to my surroundings and handled my jobs. I worked with different partners until I found a guy who was really nice and cared about folks, so we agreed to work together.

Throughout my time at the 46th Precinct, I was witness to many occasions where police officers displayed abuse of authority. Things would get ugly pretty fast. In the academy, officers are taught how to de-escalate situations, rather than making matters worse. That training is easily forgotten. You see, when police officers are called to a scene where there is a chance that violence is inevitable, the tactical thing to do is lower the risk by remaining as calm as possible. Granted, that is very difficult to do, but I believe that the more experience an officer has patrolling the streets, the better he or she is able to handle those situations. However, when officers encounter disputes and other violence-prone situations, with a limited ability to be able to mediate in those circumstances, then all hell can break loose.

Back in the 1980's, particularly 1983, the 46th Precinct was notorious for violent crimes, and numerous arrests were made on a daily basis. I have seen officers shove, punch, kick and beat civilians with their nightsticks. It was my perception that those actions were totally unnecessary. As a female rookie, I felt intimidated by the guys, and I was probably afraid of what might happen if I stood in their way to protect the safety of some of the ones who had been arrested.

Police community relations were tense as crime rose in the predominately Hispanic and African American neighborhoods. I was learning to adjust to the different hours and occasionally, I would be assigned to foot patrol where I had the opportunity to get to know the neighborhood.

After about six months, I became a bit more comfortable working different shifts with my partner. He was gentle and treated people decently. We were both Puerto Ricans and shared much in common. He didn't abuse his authority like others in the precinct. We worked well together except, my partner had horrible eating habits, was extremely overweight and loved to drink orange sodas during the midnight shifts. Oh, and he had really bad body odor. I couldn't take it anymore, I mean he was a nice guy but I just couldn't deal with all of his habits.

We had each other's back on the streets, but I couldn't help but think that if presented with a situation where he had to chase someone, it would end badly for him. I made an excuse as to why I couldn't continue to work with with him any longer and we decided to split up. He told me he understood and we parted ways. I worked with different officers (called floating)in the radio car, cruising different areas (sectors), in the precinct.

I handled car accidents, homicides, robberies, domestic violence, teenage runaways, and other police functions. When my partners and I were not directly involved in a situation we would drive around our assigned sector or area, looking for suspicious activities or suspicious persons. After driving around for eight hours we would be able to spot any unusual activity, and therefore take action if necessary.

I remember driving around the sector with an officer that I didn't know at all, and we were called to a domestic dispute. When we arrived to the apartment, I noticed an African American female yelling at us to remove her boyfriend from her apartment. All of a sudden, the officer (my partner) grabbed the male by the collar, pinned him against the wall nearly choking him, before the guy had a chance to say anything. I noticed that the man was trying to speak but instead could only stutter. He was not resisting the officer in any way. I thought that action to be very disturbing, and at the end of my shift I refused to work with him any longer.

A few years later, when I was no longer working in the precinct, that same officer was charged with applying a choke hold on a young man, killing him, following a dispute about a basketball hitting the officer's patrol car. The young man that was killed was Anthony Baez, he was 19 years old. Choke holds are not sanctioned by the city of New York, however the State of New York does allow its use.

Without getting too deep into this scenario, I can say that the officer was not threatened in any way with physical injury, but something triggered him to become abusive without any cause.

This visceral response is happening today where officers lose control, become angry and frustrated, and allow aggressive feelings to control their decisions. I am not referring to a life and death situation, I am referring to incidences where the officer has a reasonable suspicion, or the situation is not elevated at that point, or the offender is trying to escape, but not posing an immediate threat to that officer.

I am in no way insinuating that the police department is, or was, unaware of what was occurring in various parts of the city. In fact, the launching of several units such as the Human Relations Unit, Community Patrol Officer Program (CPOP), as well as the Community Affairs Division was implemented to deal with various non-emergency community problems that stressed most neighborhoods. Those units were also developed in the hopes that police community relations would improve by addressing critical issues.

I have witnessed many other situations, where handcuffed arrestees would be assaulted by more than one officer for whatever reason. This was a problem I thought would eventually worsen, if action was not immediately taken by the higher echelon. I must admit that I was fearful of reporting such incidences for fear of some kind of retaliation by my fellow officers.

Police brutality is rampant across this country, and if law enforcement agencies are not educated in cultural sensitivity, we will then witness more of the same. Mandatory training should be offered on a biannual basis to keep officers current on the cultural diversity of the communities they patrol and have sworn to protect.

Now, the flip side of that coin is that communities need educating as well. Respecting authority is one aspect that is lacking within most communities especially from younger individuals. The saying "it takes a village to raise a child," holds true for me, as I am a firm believer that education first takes place in the home, and if we don't teach our children to respect authority, then we create a pathway for insolent or criminal behavior.

There is research regarding the connection between poverty and criminal activity which unfortunately holds true, however, when both law enforcement and communities join together to meet the educational and cultural needs of those most at risk, may actually help raise awareness and alleviate criminal activity.

I decided I would leave patrol, and seek an investigations unit where I would work regular hours and perhaps make a difference.

CHAPTER 5

Neighborhood Stabilization Unit (NSU)

~~~

Neighborhood Stabilization Unit or NSU8, is where I first began my law enforcement experience. Walking the beat encompassed solitary patrolling of streets I was both familiar with, and estranged from since childhood.

The neighborhoods I traveled as a young child and as an adult were now frequented by a young Latina uniformed officer carrying a .38 Caliber Smith and Wesson 4 inch barrel. I was assigned to foot patrol for eight months. From July 1982 until March 1983, I walked foot patrols in the 45th Precinct, 43rd Precinct and the 41st Precinct. NSU8 teams worked foot patrols during the day shift and evenings, no midnight shifts.

Eight months was an awfully long time walking foot posts. I tried to familiarize myself with the neighborhoods and business owners. I enjoyed interacting with the community and for the most part, its residents were cordial and appreciated my presence.

Wearing a bullet proof vest over a tee shirt was grueling in the summer, while providing some comfort during the winter months. There were moments when my legs would ache from so much walking, but I endured, after all, I knew I would eventually get my training in a radio car.

After eight months passed, I began training in the RMPs (Radio Motor Patrol), which I thought was pretty cool. Lights and sirens were reserved for urgent and emergency calls.

I was assigned to a FTO (Field Training Officer), who was at the brink of retirement. We cruised through the precinct neighborhoods taking calls and processing paperwork. On several occasions he would ask me if I wanted to hang out after work with the guys. I would refuse every time, and he once asked me if I was gay. To shut him up, I told him I was a single parent of an eight year old son.

I must admit I was intimidated by him, but refused to let it get the best of me. He continued day after day asking me if I wanted to go out, saying that the guys were beginning to talk about me because I wouldn't go hang out with them. I didn't care. I wanted to get home to my kid. Going out after work was the last thing on my mind.

I felt harassed, but what could I do? Who could I turn to? I was so new at this, and was trying to stay alive as I patrolled the streets.

I turned my attention to the comfort of being inside a patrol car protected from bad weather. I decided I was going to ignore my training officer, and concentrate on how to handle my jobs.

I was taught in the Police Academy to expect the unexpected.

At the time, I was the only female in my NSU squad. Everyone in my squad walked a foot post all over the Bronx. We had to use public transportation to get to our assignments and most of the time the guys would ride the bus as a group, isolating themselves from me as we rode the same bus or train.

The whole physical isolation thing was a nonverbal way of telling me that they did not welcome me into their group. Socially speaking, group dynamics are intrinsic to the respective group, and commonalities are the glue that keeps the group cohesive, however it was clear to me that I did not belong. The guys did not embrace my presence. Not that I needed them to, but to a civilian, police are viewed as an entity that protects its own. That perspective is a farce and holds no truth. There is as much sexism and racism as any other organization existing today. One of the differences is that the act of segregation is at times transparent to police officers, but obscured from the public. Women continue to be harassed, threatened, coerced, intimidated, and discriminated against in many law enforcement agencies. To the point I believe, that they are afraid to speak up against corruption, abuse of authority, harassment and countless other offenses.

In the mid 1980's, the police department did not have a large number of high ranking female officers.

I can say that I wasn't motivated to take a promotional exam because, simply put, I was trying to figure my way around the job. Very few female Hispanic and African American women took promotional exams, making the pool selection even smaller. I thought perhaps it was due to the fact that some female cops would eventually want to have children, and may decide to leave the job to raise their families. One thing is for sure, law enforcement does make it difficult for moms, due to fluctuating shifts, but that doesn't mean that we can't do the job, it just makes it more difficult.

CHAPTER 6

The Police Academy From Maggot to Police Officer

"Hurry up, you maggots"! "Double-time! *Move!!!*"

That's how recruits were spoken to during the physical fitness training at the academy. In the beginning, I thought the workouts were a bit difficult, but I gradually adjusted to the rigor. We had to work out every day, and run laps around the gym. There was also some training in basic self-defense, boxing, and swimming. Men and women sweating it out together in the gym, learning how to protect each other in the event a physical confrontation with a perpetrator or a public demonstration threatening to turn violent, basically any situation that required us to take physical action.

There were some good looking dudes in the academy and really gorgeous girls, and you could almost perceive that some academy instructors had already begun fraternizing with some recruits.

The classroom lectures were rapid and intense, what with the academy lasting only six months. Final exams and a physical fitness test at the end intended to weed out the failures, and reward those who made it, by graduating them and transferring them to their training commands or precincts.

Some of the guys were cruel, insensitive and downright evil. Women had to be tough, even if they were not raised to be that way, and attending the academy was difficult enough. Meeting the physical challenges in the gym and the academic pressures in the classroom was stressful in and of itself, let alone the name calling and yelling that occurred every day.

I didn't own a car, so I took the subway every morning through rain and snow. Absences were not tolerated and "star cards" were issued out to any recruits who were tardy or late. Once a recruit received three "star cards," he or she would be reprimanded by the academy supervisors and possibly issued a command discipline, which could include dismissal from the academy.

I interpreted that action as a way of intimidating the recruit into complying with academy rules. Many times, I thought to myself that I had made a mistake and had contemplated dropping out, but didn't want to disappoint myself or my family.

The academy class that I was assigned to was huge. 2,300 recruits had been sworn in on that cold January morning in 1982, the largest class in the history of the New York City Police Department. The classes were divided into companies, and each company was overseen by a company sergeant which was usually a military veteran.

My company was Company #42. For gym, each recruit was required to wear navy blue shorts, a white tee shirt with the respective company number, and the recruit's last name printed on the back for easy identification, along with white socks and sneakers. The dress of the day was baby blue long sleeve shirt, navy clip on tie and dark blue pants with black regulation shoes. The uniforms were to be purchased from an approved police academy uniform store.

Recruits carried large black book bags issued by the academy. The large black bags included a large blue binder which contained New York City Police Department's Patrol Guide. The patrol guide would later be updated with current department memos and doubled as a study guide for promotional exams. The patrol guide, is the police officer's bible and dictates how the officers perform their duties. Furthermore, the patrol guide could be used as evidence that the officer did not follow policies and procedures when dealing with certain situations.

The guide included policies from how to dispose of dead animals found on the street, to the proper way of handling unidentified decedents.

Being a police officer is not easy, and certainly very stressful. Cops worry about criminals and the law-abiding public as well as their own co-workers. Cops are exposed to money, sex, corruption and other situations the public is not exposed to on a daily basis. Wearing that uniform gives you power and unchallenged authority. Even the FBI, CIA and other law enforcement agencies enjoy the collaborative relationships with the NYPD.

I remember cops making derogatory comments regarding the community they took and oath to protect. I recall one officer I worked with who stated to me, "Anybody you see out in the street after dark is an animal, or a criminal." He would say this as we stood near a train station observing folks getting on and off the train. These people would be walking to their homes or going to the store. Some of the guys viewed the communities they swore to protect as the enemy.

Culturally unaware white cops would patrol African American and Latino communities, while abuse of authority was the act of the day! Often times, the media took advantage of the tension between some communities and the police.

There was a time when racial tensions arose in Brooklyn, between the Hasidic and West -Indian groups. Cops slept in city buses in an effort to maintain the peace between both groups. There was no cultural awareness or sensitivity by the police department. Frankly, the bosses did not know how to handle these types of situations.

That overnight scenario was like a stand-off between the two groups. We were placed there as a show of authority, but I wasn't sure that we would be successful at maintaining peace as there was so much hatred between the two cultures. This standoff resulted after two black children of Guyanese descent were struck by a car driven by a Hasidic Jew in the Crown Heights section of Brooklyn in 1991. Following that accident that left one child dead, a two day riot followed where police officers from all over the city were pulled in to keep the situation under control.

There were so many days where I felt like putting in my early retirement papers, because of the lack of respect I felt I was getting from my male counterparts. There were other women who felt the same way, but didn't know where to turn to for help.

I recall that back in 1986, I was assigned to the Recruitment Retention Unit. I was engaged and planning my upcoming wedding. My supervisor was a civilian who touted his authoritative powers. When I informed him that I was getting married the summer of 1986, he replied to me that he had the "power to cancel my vacation." That's the kind of shit that was going on in the department.

I heard of the Police Woman's Endowment Association and reached out to the organization for their assistance. The organization intervened, and I was able to go on vacation and get married. Still, that experience left a bad taste in my mouth. I felt intimidated and fearful as I learned more about the job and what my role was within the organization.

The sexism started way back during the application process. You see, in order to become a New York City police officer, you have to pass a three part of exam. The first is a physical, the second part is a medical exam and the third section of the process is a psychological exam. When I went for my physical exam, I was up to the challenge, since I had been training on my own time. I would run alongside the cemetery on Bainbridge Avenue in the Bronx.

I would go out every day to try and build up my endurance. The physical exam consisted of running three flights of stairs in less than five minutes, dragging a 175 pound dummy and scaling five-foot wall. I completed all three effortlessly. One thing I was sure of, I was in excellent shape. At 5'7" I weighed in at 142 pounds.

When I reported to the police department doctor, I was told that I would have to be placed on review due to an abnormal curvature of my spine. I knew that was crap, because I had spent my high school years in dance and Jiu Jitsu classes. I had to wait a whole month to go back to see another department doctor who told me he did not see anything wrong with my spine, and gave me his stamp of approval. I had the impression that the police department was trying to eliminate some police department applicants, mainly females, African Americans and Latinos. The psychological exam went well. It consisted of a series of repetitious questions which I answered in a consistent manner.

Some of the women faced many challenges in the academy, poor physical shape, and not being accustomed to having to study every day while meeting family and other personal obligations.

The academy lasted for six months making study time demanding and rigorous.

The instructors were police officers assigned to the academy and the majority, were white males. I was convinced that having females in the police department was a concept not well received by upper management. Nonetheless, it is illegal to discriminate against hiring of females or other minorities into a civil service position.

Intimidation was one of the methods used by upper management to keep the recruits in line. When recruits arrived late for roll call, they would be issued a "star card," an index card used to obtain signatures of supervisors, and if a recruit earned three or more of those signatures, a command discipline would be issued. A command discipline ranged from a written admonishment to termination depending on the severity of the situation.

Recruits were yelled at, ridiculed, and made fun of if we didn't measure up to the physical demands placed on us. This was the treatment of the day and we grew accustomed to the yelling and screaming. If a recruit fell out of the run due to cramps, nausea, vomiting or shin splints, they would have to stand in the middle while recruits ran in a wide circle around them.

Instructors would then yell out "You want a partner like this on the streets?" "You're gonna get killed out there!"

Oddly enough the yelling and taunts would work to fuel us and we would get our second wind and push it to the end. We would probably run close to five miles around the academy gym. After our run we would line up for roll call and head on to the showers. It was the same routine five days a week for six months until graduation.

Driver Training

Driver training was conducted in Brooklyn where we drove around various obstacles at high speeds. That part was easy for me as I had been driving for five years prior to attending the academy. There were other recruits however who had just gotten their licenses and were having a hard time passing the course.

I thought it was kind of fun and I passed the course with no problem while others were held back.

Rodman's Neck

Firearms training took place in a location near Orchard Beach in the Bronx, called Rodman's Neck, the location way in the back, far from traffic and people. The grounds were designed to train police officers from all over the city units on the use of handguns, shotguns and rifles. We were taught to shoot at targets at close range from three feet to twenty feet.

There was also a makeshift house where simulated scenarios were played out by us and we had to make quick life or death decisions sometimes shooting each other by mistake instead of the perpetrator. We would then critique our actions with the range instructor.

At the end of that training we would qualify with our firearms and that would complete our training. Once a year every single police officer in the entire police department including high ranking officers were required to attend firearms training if we were to keep our weapons. Failure to attend the yearly mandatory firearms qualification resulted in the removal of your weapon.

To sum it all up for you, the police academy was rigorous, intense but short. When the six months were up, we had one of the largest police academy graduation class in history of the New York City Police Department and after a weekend off, each officer received orders to report to various precincts throughout the city. It was truly a wonderful day as families piled in to the Madison Square Garden for the ceremony.

Shoot To Stop

Police officers are taught to shoot to stop, not kill intentionally. That's what the public needs to understand. I believe that the majority of police officers are decent people putting their lives on the line every time they go out into the streets. The public view is quite the opposite due to the media frenzy that occurs every time there's a shooting.

Police officers work under stressful situations all of the time. They never know how things are going to turn out during a domestic dispute or a car accident or even a burglary. Police sometimes are pressured into making arrests for political reasons. It is my humble opinion that police officers truly have a desire to help people, alleviate fears and basically care about people. However, be that as it may, there are some individuals who have their own agendas and choose a law enforcement career to carry out their plan no matter what that may be.

Then, there are the citizens police officers have sworn to protect which would not only include the law abiding one but the potential or actual criminal. So it becomes sort of a Catch-22 situation. Now while in training, recruits are told that in all probability if an officer has not had to use his or her weapon in the first ten years, most likely they will not for the rest of their career. That held true for many of us.

What the public needs to understand among many things, is that uniformed officers (sometimes they work undercover), are exposed targets for those intending to cause injury or death. They can't always perceive danger making it difficult to assess situations quickly. Many times there is no time to think logically and the best decision has to be made at the time.

For example, if the officer fears for his or her life or the life of another, deadly force can, and probably will, have to be used.

Now you might think to yourself, where do police officers draw the line between abuse of authority and a justified action? Well it's subjective, what one person might interpret as a life threatening situation might not have the same meaning to another. However, I would think that if someone were trying to take your life, limb or liberty I think you would define that action as meriting some emergent response of some type.

Our judicial system attempts to act fairly regarding police incidences however, there are many individuals who feel that the courts tend to mitigate these situations. I tend to agree as we have seen numerous situations of what I believe to be unjustified shootings and abuse of authority go to trial and oftentimes, the officer(s) involved would not face any incarceration.

These situations are confronting us even more today and there is no relief in sight, unless community leaders take a more proactive approach to learning, as well as teaching respect for authority for one thing.

Having said that, law enforcement agencies and high ranking officials need to take a look at their policing policies, teach officers how to respect communities for it is a two-way street, maintain cultural sensitivity awareness in the form of a yearly mandatory class, and maintaining continuous dialogue with communities regarding priority safety issues.

The issue can be resolved, but I think we have let it fester for too long, and now both police and communities are fed up with the disparities and inequities that plight many cities.

Perception Is Everything

What you see is not always what is occurring. As a law enforcement officer, I had to develop the ability to discern situations that would ultimately affect my decision to do the right thing. As I mentioned earlier, situations are very difficult to judge first hand taking into consideration other variables.

While police officers are held to a higher standard, human error can, and will always play a part in the officer's capacity to take control of a situation before it turns violent.

We have seen all too often, officers misjudging situations, for example opening fire on an individual who is attempting to escape, or beating an individual while handcuffed, or using a Taser on an individual who is not resisting arrest.

What makes these officers respond in such a manner? Is it frustration, racism or ignorance? Is there truly intent to cause death?

I've seen individuals run from officers and when caught, brutally beaten simply because the officers had to chase them. I am not excusing this behavior, and because I have seen much of it, I chose to find another home within the New York City Police Department.

No Law Against Having an Attitude

I've always wondered why our communities display a negative perspective toward the police. Attitude is paramount to anyone's job. I'm speaking of a positive attitude. It's not as easy as it sounds however. A cop with a nice attitude is indeed hard to find and the public as well as officers would perceive the cop as weak, but I don't believe this to be so.

Attitude on the job should be as flexible as the situation the officer finds himself or herself in. Unless someone's life or limb is at risk, I believe the situation can be contained and controlled. But when aggression is used before judging the situation, then chances are that situation will turn deadly.

It was easy for me to allow myself to become angry with anyone regardless of their race, religion or socio-economic background. Many situations angered me but not to the point that I would use deadly force on someone. The stress of dealing with victims and criminals can wreak havoc on a young officer not accustomed to such brutality by cops as well as civilians, yet given a few years of exposure to that type of behavior, the officer is at risk of behaving the same way.

Now don't get me wrong, the New York City Police Departments do have units where police officers go to different communities and try to bridge gaps, but not all cities have, or are willing to implement those resources. Perhaps they are giving up. Regardless of the reason, both law enforcement and various groups of interest must come together and brainstorm a solution.

The Blue Wall of Silence (Is There Really Such a Thing?)

Because of the nature of the job, law enforcement officers form close-knit relationships which can last for years, even after retirement. Imagine riding in a radio car for eight hours a day, five days a week with someone, you're bound to become as close as a married couple, minus the sex. That doesn't mean that partners didn't have sexual relationships though. Many romantic relationships bloomed from partnerships on patrol.

It is natural to have a certain amount of loyalty for a partner, especially since officers share many experiences while on patrol and feelings of trust are established between the two. The partnership goes beyond comradery. No wonder when times get really tough officers stick together for self-protection, trust, and sometimes even fear.

Even in times where police officers are wrong in their actions towards the public, they tend to side with one another as they seek to justify even the worst case scenarios. I'm not excusing poor performance behaviors at all, just attempting to provide a reason for the behavior.

I believe there is a Code of Silence, call it a Blue Wall if you want, others may define it as loyalty, or commitment. I'm sure these days female police officers are a part of that concept, through intimidation and silence. They unknowingly are participants, as I was back in the 1980s.

Because law enforcement is a predominantly male oriented job, women do feel as though they are not as regarded or given the respect they deserve. And, still to this day are subjected to some form of sexism or another, be it blatant or subtle, but are too intimidated to rock the boat, so to speak.

My hope is that as more women enter law enforcement, they find support, encouragement and strength from their brother officers so that they can help bring a positive change in our communities. Furthermore, bringing improved job performance, perform their jobs of truly protecting the public free from intimidation and pressure from their male counterparts.

Epilogue

*Y*ou have just completed reading the "Memoirs of Women in Blue: The Good, The Bad and No Longer Silent." As you have read, both Mickey See-Asia and Raven have expounded on the memories and experiences that they encountered during their tenure as New York City Police Officers and Detectives.

It became their desire to write this memoir about their experiences after viewing, national media coverage of the numerous killings of unarmed persons over the past decade by various officers within nationwide police municipalities.

One commonality these women observed from the recent killings by police officers, to the killings that took place during their tenure as officers in the 1980's through the 2000's, was that there is a definite need for change of mindset, attitude, and continuous diversified training and interacting with the people that the officers serve in their various communities. There is also a training needed on how to interact with others within your own police municipality, regardless of your rank and title.

The "Blue Wall of Silence," "Blue Code" and/or "Blue Shield," should never be a discussion amongst any officers, because the oath that officers took was never about the deviance or loyalty amongst police officers within the police municipality that they work for. The oath was taken to protect and serve the people in the communities in which the officers serve.

The first step is that the police department has to acknowledge that the "Blue Wall of Silence" is an issue.

If you are an officer with the mindset that you must uphold and protect an officer that you know has done something that is not in accordance to the law, and you condone that officer's actions or behaviors by not addressing the behaviors with the officer, or reporting the officer, then you are just as guilty as that officer who is doing the wrongdoing. If you are not part of the solution, then you are part of the problem. The training needs to start from the top of the police municipalities to the newest officer hired in that agency.

Change Has To Come From Within.

We also believe that as communities become more cultural, diversity training should be offered to members in the community as well via the various police municipalities and community patrol officers. Implementation of constant positive interaction with the Officers that patrol the communities and the people in the communities is sorely needed. At present, people of color have great concerns for their safety and the safety of their love ones while in the presence of Police Officers.

Authors Biography

Mickey See-Asia is a native New Yorker, born in Manhattan and raised in Brooklyn. She currently resides in Florida.

She has served a total of approximately 30+ years as a Law Enforcement Officer, as well as serving as an Investigator for various police and state municipalities.

Mickey has also been a child advocate for many years, as a big sister, mentor, role, model, mother, foster parent, Child Investigator and Children's Case Manager.

She still works in the capacity of serving and assisting people. Mickey is an Independent Travel Agent sharing and meeting the needs of those who love to travel.

Mickey has her son, daughter-in-law, grandchildren, brothers, numerous Godson's and Goddaughter's, family, extended family and friends that all support her.

Raven is a retired 20-year veteran detective from the New York City Police Department.

A native New Yorker, she earned an Associate Degree of Science from Bronx Community College, a Bachelors Degree of Science in Nursing from Florida Atlantic University and a Master's Degree of Science in Nursing Education from University of Phoenix.

She is currently the Assistant Dean of Academic Success at a nursing college in Florida. There she resides with her husband of 30 years. Together they have three children and five grandchildren.

Made in the USA
Lexington, KY
24 May 2017